THE BEST OF
THE BEST OF BROCHURE DESIGN

ROCKPORT

THE BEST OF
THE BEST OF BROCHURE DESIGN

GLOUCESTER MASSACHUSETTS

ROCKPORT PUBLISHERS

First published in the United States of America by
Rockport Publishers, Inc.
33 Commercial Street
Gloucester, Massachusetts 01930-5089
Telephone: (978) 282-9590
Fax: (978) 283-2742
www.rockpub.com

Library of Congress Cataloging-in-Publication data available

ISBN 1-56496-922-3

10 9 8 7 6 5 4 3 2

Layout: Susan Raymond
Cover Design: Hatmaker
      Creative Director: Christian Goveia
      Senior Designer: Prang Tharawanich

Printed in China

CONTENTS

with Bernard L. H

RIL 25th
ATURDAY
8:30 - 5:00

HALL

OR.

PING ROOM

UP

ITECTURALL

l Heritage Program of th

INTRODUCTION

Brochure design is one of the few areas of design that designers of all levels and types create. It is one of the consistent, bread-and-butter areas of the design business and as such, is a constant challenge to the creativity of even the best designers. How do you offer a client a new and innovative brochure concept that meets their business goals when the consumer is already saturated by the millions of brochures that are in the market? What makes a brochure special? It's not just the product or service itself that makes a brochure effective, but the presentation of the brochure that makes people notice it, keep it around, and pull it out when needed.

With its publication of the Best of Brochure Design series, Rockport
has celebrated the graphic art of brochure design for many years.
In creating each of the books in this series, Rockport has asked
designers from around the world to submit their best recent brochure
design work. Top designers have been asked to judge and select the
final submissions for each book. The series is now seven volumes
strong and has showcased thousands of examples of the best of
brochure design from the top international designers, hundreds of
new designers, and in-house company design departments alike.

In this volume Rockport has culled from the thousands of brochure
designs that have been selected and published over the years to give
you *the best of the best* in one complete volume. A tribute to the art
of the brochure and a celebration of great design, this is a unrivaled
collection.

第三十四届国际家俱展览会瓦伦西亚

会瓦伦西亚

届国际家俱展览

第三十四

流等家設計的各種型號的牆面裝飾板，以及為"高巨巳重于"愛女老莉俱的各種桃桃。展屏控其古典式，琦代

流行式，表面精裝型和鄉村風格的秩序面設計布置，當然還包括古典的 Boulevard 林陰路式和 Gallery 畫廊式

的家具精選；第七展廳將為您展示更加豪華的古典《和田園風格的佳作；最后一個展廳名為先鋒者展廳，再一次

和 SIDI 國際室內裝璜設計沙龍聯合，為您嶄露當今家具設計佼佼者的集翠。

短短的六天，一年僅一次。瓦倫西亞將熱誠地歡迎您光顧這一家具大世界。

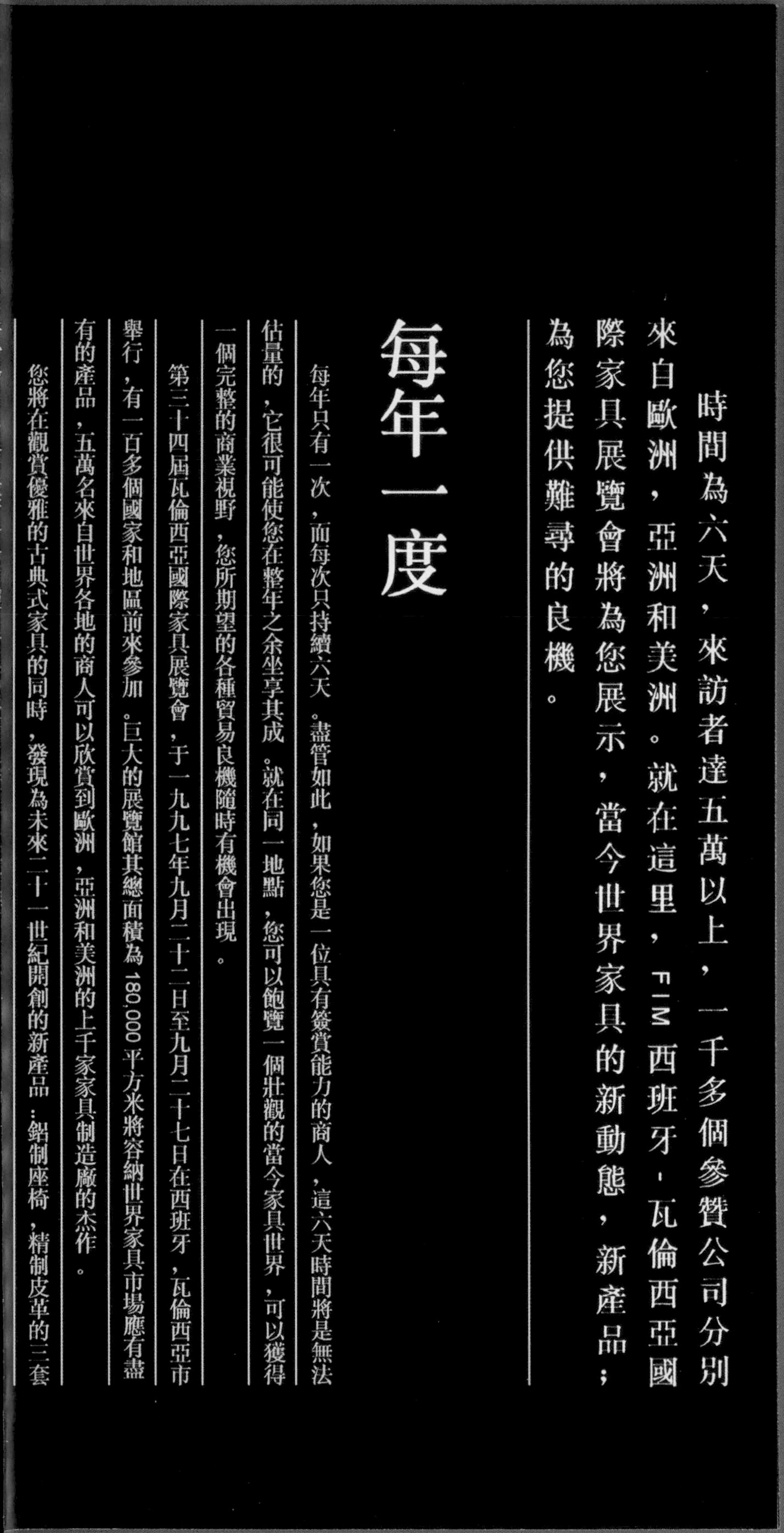

時間為六天，來訪者達五萬以上，一千多個參贊公司分別
來自歐洲，亞洲和美洲。就在這里，FIM西班牙-瓦倫西亞國
際家具展覽會將為您展示，當今世界家具的新動態，新產品；
為您提供難尋的良機。

每年一度

每年只有一次，而每次只持續六天。盡管如此，如果您是一位具有簽賞能力的商人，這六天時間將是無法
估量的，它很可能使您在整年之余坐享其成。就在同一地點，您可以飽覽一個壯觀的當今家具世界，可以獲得
一個完整的商業視野，您所期望的各種貿易良機隨時有機會出現。
第三十四屆瓦倫西亞國際家具展覽會，于一九九七年九月二十二日至九月二十七日在西班牙，瓦倫西亞市
舉行，有一百多個國家和地區前來參加。巨大的展覽館其總面積為180.000平方米將容納世界家具市場應有盡
有的產品，五萬名來自世界各地的商人可以欣賞到歐洲，亞洲和美洲的上千家家具制造廠的杰作。
您將在觀賞優雅的古典式家具的同時，發現為未來二十一世紀開創的新產品：鋁制座椅，精制皮革的三套

DESIGN FIRM | Pepe Gimeno, S.L.
DESIGNER | Pepe Gimeno
CLIENT | Feria Internacional del Mueble de Valencia
TOOLS | Macromedia FreeHand, Adobe Photoshop
PRINTING PROCESS | Offset

This is the program given out at the International
Furniture Fair in Valencia. The brochure had to be
designed in five different languages.

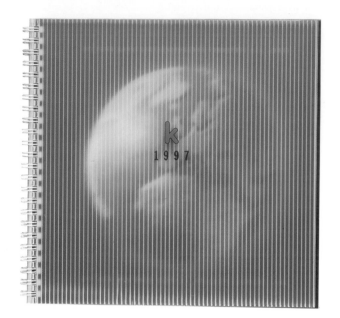

DESIGN FIRM | Q DESIGN
ART DIRECTORS | Thilo Von Debschitz, Laurenz Nielbock
DESIGNER | Roman Holt
CLIENT | VKE
TOOLS | QuarkXPress, Adobe Photoshop
PAPER | Akylux & Polyart
PRINTING PROCESS | Ultraviolet, four-color Pantone

Annual Report for VKE (association of plastic processing industries). Text and cover is all synthetic paper, therefore UV-printing was used.

Geschäftsbereich

ÖFFENTLICHKEITSARBEIT

Der VKE sucht auch in seiner Öffentlichkeitsarbeit die Zusammenarbeit mit anderen europäischen Verbänden, wo immer sich eine Möglichkeit dazu ergibt. So wurde im vergangenen Jahr auf Initiative des VKE ein gemeinsames, einheitliches europäisches Logo für Kunststoff auf den Weg gebracht. Es soll als Siegel für den innovativen, vielseitigen Werkstoff der Zukunft stehen und für alle Europäer leicht verständlich sein. Gerade im Bereich der Kommunikation macht multinationale Zusammenarbeit besonderen Sinn: Internationaler Handel und ungehinderter, reger Informationsaustausch auf verschiedensten Kommunikationskanälen haben längst auch die Massenkommunikation internationalisiert.

Das gilt im besonderem Maß fürs Internet. Der Datenhighway kennt keine Ländergrenzen.

Seit dem Frühsommer 1997 zeigt auch der VKE mit professionell gestalteten, eigenen Seiten im Internet Flagge. Unter „www.vke.de" finden sich Basisinformationen rund um Kunststoff und die Kunststoff-Industrie ebenso wie aktuelle News aus der Welt der Polymere – selbstverständlich auf deutsch und auf englisch. Zahlreiche Links, also per Mausklick herstellbare, direkte Verbindungen, runden das Angebot ab. Von der VKE-Homepage gelangt man problemlos zu den Mitgliedsfirmen, zu Organisationen und anderen Kunststoff-Verbänden, auch im europäischen Ausland und sogar in Übersee. Und die Nutzungsstatistik zeigt, daß gerade die europäischen Nachbarn eifrige Websurfer sind. Nur etwas über die Hälfte der Homepage-Besucher kam aus Deutschland.

Ein Highlight auf den Webseiten war im vergangenen Jahr die europäische Online-Regatta, ein gemeinsam mit den europäischen Kunststoff-Erzeugern entwickeltes Spiel im Internet. Die User konnten von der VKE-Seite zu verschiedenen großen Kunststoff-Anwendern surfen, Fragen zu Kunststoff beantworten und damit attraktive Preise gewinnen. Hauptgewinn war ein Segeltörn mit Wibke Bülle und Nicola Birkner, den Seglerinnen der 470er Olympia-Crew, die unter dem Motto „Innovation in Kunststoff" an den Start gehen.

Sponsoring: Sport und Kultur

Denn auch das 1996 begonnene Sponsoring der Seglerinnen der 470er Klasse und des deutschen Frauen-Nationalachters wird fortgesetzt. Die Partnerschaft

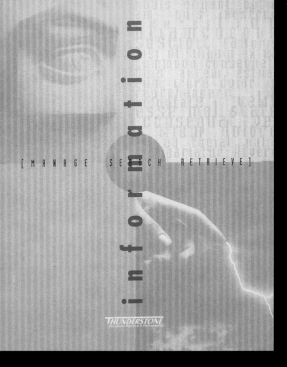

information

[MANAGE SEARCH RETRIEVE]

THUNDERSTONE

DESIGN FIRM | Zylstra Design and Denise Kemper Design
(collaboration)

ART DIRECTORS | Melinda Zylstra, Denise Kemper

DESIGNERS | Melinda Zylstra, Denise Kemper

PHOTOGRAPHER | Stock

COPYWRITER | Thunderstone

CLIENT | Thunderstone

TOOLS | QuarkXPress

PAPER | Neenah Environment Mesa White,
UV Ultra II Columns

PRINTING PROCESS | Three-color offset lithography

The design firm's goal was to create a unique
brochure that stands out from the crowd and
reflects the client's non-traditional outlook.
With this goal in mind, they designed the project
using unusual page layout, paper stock, and
photographic images.

THUNDERSTONE?

Thunderstone is an independent R&D company that provides high-end software to manage, retrieve, filter and electronically publish information content consisting of text and multimedia. Over the last 17 years Thunderstone has sold more than 400,000 end-user licenses to corporations, software developers, content providers and government entities. Privately held, Thunderstone maintains a constant commitment to excellence and innovation within diverse areas of information management and retrieval. Its focus on constant technical advancement provides its customers with the ability to specifically address the demands of their user base without compromise.

THE THUNDERSTONE DIFFERENCE

Large organizations generally have specific information retrieval and management needs that can only be met by a combination of several unrelated products, but this type of integration is time consuming and error prone. Other retrieval vendors just index text and provide the ubiquitous list of answers. Thunderstone will realize and implement the entirety of the application exactly as envisioned; rapidly and maintainably. Our Texis RDBMS is fully capable of managing text and multimedia objects out of the box without the need to resort to loosely coupled "Data-Blade" programs. The Thunderstone infrastructure can meet the diverse and unique needs for almost any internet application.

The marketplace for internetworked information management/retrieval systems is rapidly expanding. Texis represents a crucial part of the information requirement by symmetrically merging objects, relational data, and full text retrieval. Thunderstone has been a pioneer since 1984 with the first concept based retrieval product on the market. No other product can make this claim, and no integration of other products can easily replicate Texis' functionality.

www.thunderstone.com
[SEARCH CLASSIFY DISSEMINATE]

DESIGN FIRM | Stoltze Design
ART DIRECTOR | Clifford Stoltze
DESIGNERS | Clifford Stoltze, Dina Radeka
PHOTOGRAPHER | William Huber
CLIENT | New England Investment Company
PAPER | Mohawk 50/10, Champion Benefit Oyster
80 lb. text, Gilclear Medium 28 lb.
PRINTING PROCESS | Cover: 4 PMS plus varnish; front
section: 5 PMS plus varnish;
financials: 1 PMS

DESIGN FIRM | JD Thomas Company
DESIGNER | Clive Piercey
PHOTOGRAPHERS | Various/Stock
COPYWRITER | Jim Thomas
CLIENT | Peerless Lighting Corporation
TOOLS | QuarkXPress, Adobe Photoshop
PAPER | French-Construction 100 lb. cover
PRINTING PROCESS | Four-color offset

This quarterly publication was created to announce new technologies and products. The distinctive design is meant to appeal to interior designers and architects.

WALL & COVE

LIGHTDUCT™ and LIGHTFIN™ WALL-MOUNTED FIXTURES use the same advanced HOT-5™ technology and optical system to project soft, uniform light on the wall above and across the ceiling in corridors, small offices, rooms with low ceilings, and in general use areas.

Compared with similar T8 and T5 systems, the performance is extraordinary. Single-lamp Diminutive wall-mounted fixtures project nearly as much light as 2-lamp conventional fixtures, allowing you to decrease the number of lamps while also reducing ongoing maintenance and energy costs.

The sleek housings match Lightfin and Lightduct pendant-mounted designs, and feature the same high quality materials, finish and construction.

DIMINUTIVE COVE LIGHTING can transform a ceiling into a glowing surface that provides pure, diffuse light virtually free of hot spots, glare and shadow. Combining HOT-5™ technology and the same sophisticated optics, the system projects continuous levels of illumination from fewer lamps, and is scaled down to install easily into smaller architectural spaces.

6"x 2" Diminutive Cove lighting features a patented optical system inside a compact, easy-to-install housing that fits into smaller architectural cavities.

A Diminutive indirect lighting scheme offers exceptional space design versatility. In addition to pendant-mounted fixture arrangements, you can extend the sleek new look into small offices and conference rooms, corridors and waiting areas using matching wall-mounted fixtures (shown here at Peerless Design & Technology Center). You can also add dramatic cove lighting in selected special use spaces.

Lighting engineer: Erik Conroy Photographer: John Sutton

Wall-mounted and cove systems *extend* the Diminutive look.

DIMINUTIVE DIMINUTIVE DIMINUTIVE DIMINUTIVE **DIMINUTIVE** DIMINUTIVE DIMINUTIVE DIMINUTIVE DIMINUTIVE DIMINUTIVE DIMINUTIVE DIMINUTIVE **DIMINUTIVE** DIMINUTIVE DIMI

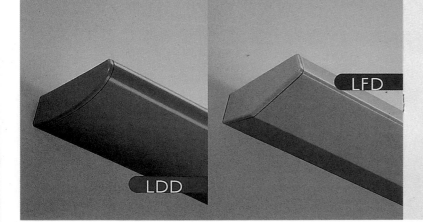

LFD

LDD

An *important word* about warranties:

To assure maximum return on your investment, Diminutive fixtures are shipped with lamps included and warranted by Peerless. Separately, when using Osram/Sylvania lamps and ballasts, Osram/Sylvania's Quick 60+ warranty program covers lamps for two years and ballasts for five years, with convenient on-site professional support from Sylvania Lighting Services.

Note:

The computer-intense environment of ECHOSTAR Corporation's headquarters in Littleton, Colorado was among the first to be lit by Peerless Lightfin HOT-5 fixtures. The firm and its architect, burkettdesign, Denver, are happy with how the small-scaled fixtures add an attractive design element without intruding into the space. The engineers, ABS Consultants, like how Lightfin meets the challenge of extraordinarily high ceilings with fewer fixtures and lamps than the conventional 3-lamp T8 alternative. RPs criteria, lighting levels, and ceiling uniformity standards were easily satisfied.

Lighting engineers: Dennis Fazio, Justin Kerns Photographer: Rich Douglas

To Finish Line, Inc. image was vital in the design of its corporate headquarters in Indianapolis. Parabolic lighting was thus considered inappropriate, yet conventional T-8 indirect lighting appeared bulky because of 8–10' ceiling heights. Lightduct answered with diminutive fixtures spaced 30' on center, delivering over 50 initial fc with 7-to-1 ceiling uniformity ratio. 20% fewer fixtures were required, and energy lamping and installation costs were significant reduced.

Architect: Wolfson-Young Corporation Electrical engineer: Marks Levy Associates Photographer: Richard Seaton

行史簡介

總行

● 中國銀行的前身是一九零五年清朝政府成立的戶部銀行，一九零八年改稱大清銀行。一九一二年一月，奉孫中山臨時大總統談論，改組為中國銀行，同年二月在上海開業。一九四九年十一月，中國銀行總管理處遷往北京。一九五三年中央人民政府指定中國銀行為國家特許的外匯專業銀行。一九七九年國務院批准中國銀行為國務院直屬機構，專門使國家外匯外貿專業組織的職能。

● 隨著國家經濟體制改革及對外開放政策的持續深入，中國銀行進入了新的歷史發展時期，並以其雄厚的實力、卓著的信譽、穩健的經營，跨入了世界大銀行的前列，並逐步向國有商業銀行轉化。

● 根據英國《銀行家》雜誌一九九七年公佈的全球一千家大銀行中，以核心資本排名，中國銀行列世界第十五位，國內第一位；以總資產列世界第二十四位。世界著名雜誌《歐洲貨幣》連續三年評中國銀行為最佳國內銀行。

1. 1943年建成的上海中國銀行大樓營業廳
   The banking hall of our Shanghai Office in 1943
2. 中國銀行總行大廈
   The Bank of China Headquarters Building
3. 1912年中國銀行發行的鈔票
   Banknotes issued by the Bank of China in 1912
4. 1950年1月鄭鐵如經理率領分行全體職工接受中國銀行總管理處的領導
   Mr. Zheng Tieru, Branch Manager, took the lead in accepting Beijing administration in January 1950
5. 1950年3月鄭鐵如經理主為香港中國銀行大廈奠基
   Mr. Zheng Tieru officiating the Foundation-laying Ceremony of the BOC Building in March 1950

ORIGIN OF BANK OF CHINA

HEAD OFFICE

● Bank of China's predecessor in the Qing Dynasty was the Treasury Bank, which was established by the government in 1905 and subsequently renamed as the Bank of Great Qing in 1908. In January 1912, under the sanction of Dr. Sun Yat-sen, the Interim President, Bank of Great Qing was reorganized with its name changed to Bank of China. The Bank commenced its business in Shanghai in February, 1912. In November 1949, the Head Office of Bank of China was relocated to Beijing. In 1953, the Central People's Government issued a decree designating Bank of China as the state's foreign exchange bank. In 1979, the State Council decided that the Bank should be under its direct jurisdiction with specific functions of a state bank specializing in foreign exchange and foreign trade.

● China's reform and open policy has directed the Bank of China to a new historical era. With its solid foundation, fine reputation and prudent operation, the Bank has become one of the leading banks in the world, and is gradually being transformed into a state-owned commercial bank.

According to "The Banker" of July 1997, Bank of China was ranked 15th among the world's 1,000 largest banks in terms of core capital, and the first in China. With respect to total assets, the Bank was the 24th in the world. "Euromoney" also selected Bank of China as the best domestic bank in China for three consecutive years.

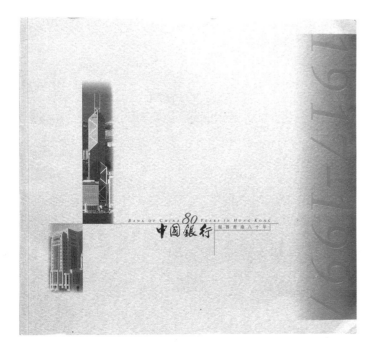

DESIGN FIRM | Kan & Lau Design Consultants
ART DIRECTORS | Kan Tai-Keung, Lau Sin Hong
DESIGNER | Cheung Lai Sheung
CLIENT | Bank of China, Hong Kong
PAPER | Cover: Hiap Moh F961-304 320 gsm;
        text: 151 gsm Artpaper and
        Heiwa Ultrafelt 118 gsm

The contrast between the new and old buildings of the Bank of China expresses the bank's progress over its eighty-year history.

DESIGNERS | Sandy Salurio, Arne Sarmiento

COPYWRITER | Fides Bernardo

CLIENT | Fil-Estate Group of Companies

TOOLS | Adobe Photoshop and PageMaker, Macromedia
FreeHand

PAPER | C2S 220 lb.

PRINTING PROCESS | Offset

This interactive sales kit includes a movable
wheel that shows the titles of the four districts
within the park. Bright, playful colors in solid
blocks readily create a feeling of outdoor fun
and excitement, clearly establishing that life in
Southwoods Ecocentrum is an everyday adventure.

Caring for and managing our land

Steward

Land was at the heart of the congressional discussions about the Alaska Native Claims Settlement Act when it was passed in 1971.

Land also provides an incredibly strong tie to our heritage for those of us who live in Southeast Alaska and for those of us who left but who still trace our ancestry to the region.

For such reasons, our maturing corporation is devoting considerable time and attention to how we care for and manage our land.

Sealaska is structuring its resource management program to perpetuate our cultural identity...

New policies at work

In 1982, Sealaska took an important step toward its stewardship mission, with the implementation of its first environmental policy. Ultimately, changing times and new laws called for a positive step ahead, resulting in even stronger policies and programs that were adopted by the corporation late last year.

Sealaska's new environmental policies require the corporation to aggressively assume respon...

Sealaska is responsible for balancing conservation and environmental considerations with...

DESIGN FIRM | Hornall Anderson Design Works, Inc.

ART DIRECTORS | Jack Anderson, Katha Dalton

DESIGNERS | Katha Dalton, Heidi Favour, Nicole Bloss, Michael Brugman

ILLUSTRATOR | Sealaska archive

COPYWRITER | Michael E. Dederer

CLIENT | Sealaska Corporation

TOOLS | Adobe PageMaker, QuarkXPress

PAPER | Quest Green, Cougar Natural, Speckletone Barn Red, Cougar Opaque, Quest Moss, Gilbert Voice Rye

The client needed a piece that would serve not only as an annual report, but would also celebrate the company's 25th anniversary. The Hornall Anderson team created a clean design, incorporating earthy colors and native art references. Their biggest challenge was printing the Pantone colors on uncoated, colored paper stock, which required multiple drawdowns.

CAMP JOHN HAY

DESIGN FIRM | The Creative Response Company, Inc.
ART DIRECTOR/DESIGNER | Arne Sarmiento
PHOTOGRAPHER | Francis Abraham
COPYWRITER | Pia Gutierrez
CLIENT | CJH Development Corporation
TOOLS | Adobe Photoshop and PageMaker,
Macromedia FreeHand
PAPER | C2S 229 lb., Matte 100 lb.
PRINTING PROCESS | Offset

To distinguish Camp John Hay from among other
land developments, a fictional character was created
whose poignant diary entries show the personal
significance of living in Baguio, the summer capital
of the Philippines.

VISION STATEMENT

To be a Group of world-class people
guided by managerial excellence.
To use our resources wisely, responsibly.
To explore, develop, and manage existing
and potential energy sources,
whenever, wherever.
All these that the country would
better place to live in
And that prosperity would br
envelop the lan
This is, this shall, fore
The Philippine Nation
Going boldly where
has ever

1994 ANNUAL REPORT

Changing with the World for the Generations to come

DESIGN FIRM | The Creative Response Company, Inc.

ALL DESIGN | Sanady Salurio

PHOTOGRAPHER | Francis Abraham

COPYWRITER | Creative Copy Team

CLIENT | Philippine National Oil Company (PNOC)

TOOLS | Adobe Photoshop and PageMaker,
Macromedia FreeHand

PAPER | C2S 220, Matte 80 lb.

PRINTING PROCESS | Offset

The challenge for PNOC's 1995–1996 annual report
was to create a divergent approach to the usual technical presentation common to petroleum companies,
while conveying their adaptation and responsiveness
to ever-changing environments. The strategy of using
oil pastel renditions successfully met this challenge
and strengthened the company's position as a
responsible leader in the petroleum industry.

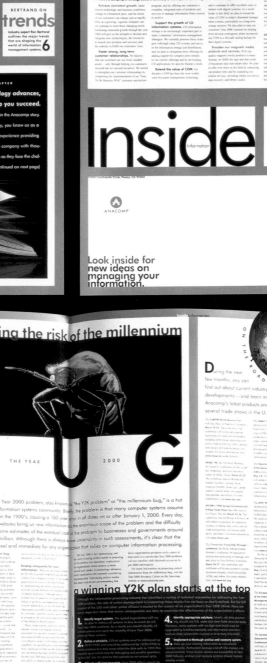

DESIGN FIRM | Mires Design

ART DIRECTOR | John Ball

DESIGNER | Deborah Hom

ILLUSTRATOR | Tracy Sabin

PHOTOGRAPHER | John Still, Michael Campos stock

COPYWRITERS | Danniel White, Steve Miller

CLIENT | Anacomp

PRINTING PROCESS | Six-color offset

Anacomp's *Inside Information* newsletter was designed to re-introduce a revitalized company to its customer base. A new logo, new products, and a new focus were created, accompanied by industry-trend stories that reinforce Anacomp's leadership position.

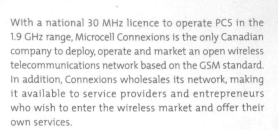

With a national 30 MHz licence to operate PCS in the 1.9 GHz range, Microcell Connexions is the only Canadian company to deploy, operate and market an open wireless telecommunications network based on the GSM standard. In addition, Connexions wholesales its network, making it available to service providers and entrepreneurs who wish to enter the wireless market and offer their own services.

Microcell's GSM network serves five regions, and currently offers digital coverage to nearly 40% of the Canadian population, and by the end of 1998, it will cover the majority of the population. Roaming on AMPS networks increases coverage to 94% of the Canadian population.

The approach is simple:

| Adopt a well-proven technology that is on the leading edge in terms of costs and product development and is a world standard.

| Build out a cost-effective network to support the economics of a mass-market approach: build in densely populated areas where people live, work and spend their leisure time; offer roaming on the cellular analog network between cities and in remote areas; offer worldwide coverage through roaming on the networks of its GSM counterparts.

| Design an open network and offer it to other providers on a wholesale basis, to quickly leverage the network investment, and capitalize on the opportunities created by additional niche and full-service operators entering this market.

In the first half of 1998, Microcell expects that the network will be rolled out progressively to an additional 3.7 million Canadians, rapidly increasing the overall population coverage. Networks will be launched in areas such as Victoria, Edmonton, Calgary and Barrie. Microcell is also working towards additional roaming services in other centres in the U.S. and overseas.

THE GSM ADVANTAGE

| GSM (GLOBAL SYSTEM FOR MOBILE COMMUNICATIONS) IS THE WORLD'S LEADING WIRELESS DIGITAL TECHNOLOGY, WITH NETWORKS OPERATING IN 109 COUNTRIES, SERVING 66 MILLION SUBSCRIBERS AT THE END OF 1997. TWO MILLION NEW GSM CUSTOMERS ARE ADDED EVERY MONTH WORLDWIDE. GSM NOW ACCOUNTS FOR 31% OF THE WORLD'S TOTAL WIRELESS MARKET. ONLY GSM HANDSETS USE A SMART CARD, CONTAINING THE CUSTOMER'S INDIVIDUAL AUTHENTICATION KEY, PERSONAL IDENTIFICATION AND SERVICE PROFILE INFORMATION. GSM OFFERS SUPERIOR VOICE QUALITY, CALL PRIVACY AND THE ADVANTAGES OF NATIONAL AND INTERNATIONAL ROAMING.

☐ CURRENT FIDO PCS COVERAGE AREA
■ ANALOG COVERAGE AREA

DESIGN FIRM | Goodhue & Associés Design Communication
CREATIVE DIRECTOR | Lise Charbonneau
ART DIRECTOR | Paulo Correia
DESIGNERS | Josée Barsalo, Aube Savard
ILLUSTRATOR | Daniel Huot
PHOTOGRAPHER | Jean-Francois Berube
COPYWRITER | Microcell Solutions Language Services
CLIENT | Microcell Telecommunications Inc.
TOOLS | QuarkXPress, Macromedia FreeHand, Infini D
PRINTING PROCESS | Offset

During 1997, the client revolutionized personal communications and experienced outstanding growth. They wished to emphasize the personnel responsible, hence the use of vibrant-yellow, human figures on the cover, and staff photos inside.

The Beresford process starts with an examination of your existing applications and architecture—your departments, users' requirements, software requirements and the like—and compares them against the Beresford Model. From here, Beresford cost-effectively provides Design, Project

MODELS CREATE THE ULTIMATE SOLUTION

Management, and Professional Skills to a successful implementation. Although implementation may differ from customer to customer, the Beresford approach will tailor the system exactly to meet your needs, while maintaining a package. You may require a phased implementation, for example, leaving some legacy systems in place while replacing others. — Beresford is a powerful system that enables you to see your loan, lease and credit card business while it is in process. The movement and flow of information can be managed throughout the day, at any moment and from any location, regardless of where it originates. —

In 1927, Charles Lindbergh made the idea of aviation technology less intimidating by being the first to fly alone and non-stop across the Atlantic Ocean from New York to Paris in a high-wing mono-plane, "The Spirit of St. Louis."

MODELS IN FLIGHT

BERESFORD

DESIGN FIRM | ZGraphics, Ltd.
ART DIRECTOR | Joe Zeller
DESIGNER | Renee Clark
ILLUSTRATOR | Paul Turnbaugh
CLIENT | Beresford

Beresford has created a comprehensive loan, lease, and credit-card system adaptable every part of any finance company. They achieve this adaptability by producing models that are customized to the target business. The concept of airplane model-building helps to convey Beresford's strategy while focusing on their theme: models in flight.

DESIGN FIRM | Television Broadcasts Limited

ART DIRECTOR | Alice Yuen-wan Wong

PRINCIPAL DESIGNER | Andrew Pong-yee Chen

DESIGNER | Tom Shu-wai Cheung

CLIENT | Miss Hong Kong Pageant 1998

TOOLS | Adobe Illustrator and Photoshop,
Macromedia FreeHand

PAPER | 150 gsm art paper

PRINTING PROCESS | Four-color plus one Pantone on cover;
four-color inside

To convey the pageant is "as glamorous as a crystal palace,"
the designers created a three-dimensional environment and
gave the pageant's logo a magical appearance.

Commercial~Free
TV for **Kids.**

Worry~Free
TV for **Parents.**

HBO
for
kids

DESIGN FIRM | SJI Associates Inc.

ART DIRECTOR | Susan Seers

DESIGNER | Karen Lemke

COPYWRITER | Jessy Vendley

CLIENT | HBO, Cindy Matero

TOOLS | QuarkXPress, Adobe Photoshop and Illustrator

PRINTING PROCESS | Offset

HBO wanted a brochure design that would promote their line-up of children's programming and give each program the space to show its own personality. The use of patterned backgrounds gave each spread its own identity, while tying the brochure together.

HBO®
for kids

Every morning 7:00-8:00 ET/PT

More than ever, parents are concerned about what their kids are exposed to on television. Which is why we created HBO for Kids—a fun,

enriching alternative to commercially driven children's programming. We don't answer to advertisers; we answer to parents. Which means HBO for Kids airs only programs that parents

can feel good about. Intelligent shows that are as educational as they are entertaining, and scheduled at sensible times so that kids of all ages can enjoy them.

...so much fun, kids don't even notice it's good for them!

DESIGN FIRM | AWG Graphics Communicação, Ltda.

ART DIRECTOR | Renata Claudia de Cristofaro

DESIGNERS | Dennys Lima, Marcello Gava

CLIENT | Reifenhäuser Ind. Maq. Ltda.

TOOLS | Adobe Photoshop, CorelDraw, PC

PAPER | Couchê 180 gsm

PRINTING PROCESS | Offset

This brochure was designed to sell plastic extrusion machinery by artistically showing the final product and its applications. To achieve this objective, the designers mixed products obtained by the machinery with the machinery itself.

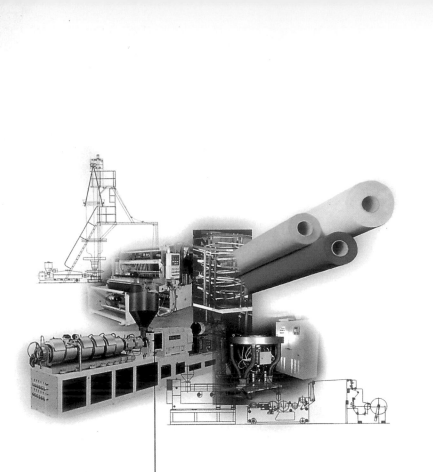

Moonlight Media puts the **power** and **potential** of online media at your service.

Skill and confidence are an unconquered army. —George Herbert, 1657

POWERFUL PARTNERSHIP Ⓔ

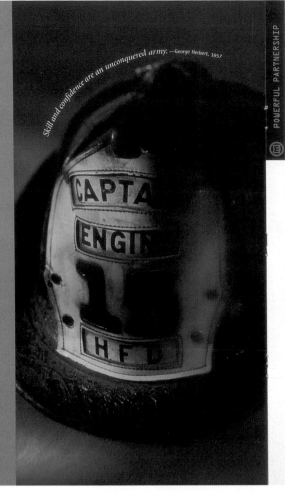

Our experienced, imaginative staff is ready to serve as your technology partner, helping you achieve your business goals with speed and efficiency. And Moonlight Media's commitment to you is ongoing. Once we design your Internet or Intranet site, we consult with you on developing your strategy and targeting your audience. And our technology experts keep you aware of emerging tools and opportunities that will prove valuable to you and the success of your business.

You see, Moonlight Media takes a handcrafted approach to handling your Internet, Intranet, and Web-based needs. And if you think "handcrafted" is an inappropriate term to describe an outfit whose stock in trade is leading-edge online technology, please keep this in mind:

Our company is not about technology. Our company is about using technology to help your company do business more successfully.

James M. Vardaman & Company

For this forestry consulting firm, Moonlight Media developed a web site that provides critical timber market information for investors, along with a private archive of timber publications that may be reviewed by authenticated site members. We also constructed a JAVA-based software tool that allows site visitors to demo the company's PTAEDA2V+ECONVR software that predicts timber yields and their associated financial returns.

Stuart C. Irby Company

Moonlight Media constructed a territory planning and reporting tool for Irby that allows outside salesmen to plan and track their weekly sales activity. Salesmen use custom Active X controls, developed by Moonlight Media, to enter their plans into the parent Call Planner database. Once entered, these plans are tracked and later married to mainframe data to generate performance reports. Managers also have the capability to log on and review the call planning activity.

MOONLIGHT MEDIA, INC.℠

Because your vision is bigger than a site.℠

DESIGN FIRM | Communication Arts Company
ART DIRECTOR/DESIGNER | Hilda Stauss Owen
PHOTOGRAPHER | Photodisc: Design Photo Image
COPYWRITER | David Adcock
CLIENT | Moonlight Media, Inc.
TOOLS | Macromedia FreeHand
PAPER | Stock Karma
PRINTING PROCESS | Four-color offset lithography

In contrast to the youthful client's high-tech enterprise of Web design and services, the designers chose a striking collection of nostalgic images that suggest tried-and-true reliability and strength.

Successful discoveries last year on the Pitchfork Ranch have resulted in daily production of 350 barrels of oil, and additional acreage is scheduled for 3D seismic surveys in 1998.

the history behind PITCHFORK RANCH

The circus partnership of Barnum & Bailey was not the only important alliance formed in 1881. Eugene Williams and Dan Gardner, boyhood friends in Mississippi before the Civil War, joined forces that year to start a cattle business on the South Wichita River near Lubbock, Texas. The last quarter of the 19th century was a rough-and-tumble time for the growing cattle industry. Surviving drought, severe winters, unstable prices and occasional rustlers, the Pitchfork Ranch held title to 97,000 acres and had increased its herd to more than 12,000 cattle by 1900.

The present-day operation, an outstanding example of perseverance, loyalty and respect for the cowboy way of life, has incorporated the modern world of helicopters and cellular phones with traditions of the past, including the historic chuckwagon, seasonal roundups and a brand that has been around since 1843. The 165,000-acre ranch in central West Texas has endured over 100 years of assorted political and economical difficulties that defeated many large cattle syndicates from ranching's Golden Era.

The descendants of Eugene Williams have been directly involved in the Pitchfork Land and Cattle Company since it was incorporated in 1883. With a century of consolidation and acquisitions, the ranch is actually larger today than at any other time in its history. Louis Dreyfus Natural Gas and Pitchfork, sharing a belief in traditional standards of trust and honesty, work together for results that are mutually beneficial to both companies.

continued from page 17 OFFSHORE This acreage position was acquired after evaluating seismic data information compiled by the Company that indicates multiple targets at depths ranging from 8,000 to 12,000 feet. Of the total $25 million budgeted for offshore drilling, $18 million, or 72 percent, is slated for exploration activities in 1998. To counter an industry shortage of offshore drilling rigs, the Company has entered into a six-month drilling rig contract with an option to extend the contract for another six months. Louis Dreyfus Natural Gas plans to drill at least five exploratory wells and has identified 11 additional prospects.

exploration, WESTERN The Permian Basin of southeast New Mexico and West Texas is another region in which Louis Dreyfus Natural Gas has committed to important exploration projects. The Company's leasehold inventory of over 1.2 million acres will yield approximately 15 exploration wells in 1998 with a focus on projects in the Midland, Val Verde and the Delaware Basins of New Mexico. Typical exploration targets are the Strawn, Morrow and Atoka, with depths ranging from 7,000 to 13,000 feet. Forty percent of the total drilling budget for the Western region will go to exploration projects.

Pitchfork Ranch continues to be a successful and promising project; the Company has exclusive exploration rights and a 78 percent working interest in 140,000 gross acres. Louis Dreyfus Natural Gas negotiated with the landowners of this working ranch in West Texas to be one of the first companies to shoot a large 3D seismic project. Following a 30-square-mile survey and four successful Tannehill discoveries last year, there are plans for at least four more exploratory wells in 1998. Knowledge gained from this shoot and from current drilling is being used to identify similar anomalies in the ranch area. The Company has plans for a new 50-square-mile 3D survey; after evaluation of this data, additional drilling is expected to begin by the fourth quarter.

exploration, MID-CONTINENT Louis Dreyfus Natural Gas properties in Oklahoma, Kansas and the Texas Panhandle represent some of its most established production. And despite the extensive amount of development in this area, exploration teams have successfully identified numerous targets, each of which has the potential for daily production levels exceeding one million cubic feet. Almost one-fourth of the $40 million total drilling budget will focus on exploratory targets, including the Watonga-Chickasha Trend which produces from the Morrow/Springer formation.

18   19

97

LOUIS DREYFUS NATURAL GAS

DESIGN FIRM | Wood Design

ART DIRECTOR | Tom Wood

DESIGNERS | Tom Wood, Alyssa Weinstein

PHOTOGRAPHER | Chris Shinn

COPYWRITER | Maryanne Costello

CLIENT | Louis Dreyfus Natural Gas

TOOLS | QuarkXPress, Adobe Illustrator

PAPER | Mohawk Navaho

PRINTING PROCESS | Six-color, die-cut

The annual report parallels the exploration and production activities of the company and the lives of the cowboys and ranchers working on the properties. The design contrasts editorial and technical attitudes through typography, journalistic photography, feature stories, color, and sequence.

DESIGN FIRM | WATCH! Graphic Design

ART DIRECTOR | Bruno Watel

DESIGNER | Tim Goldman

PHOTOGRAPHER | Hot Shots, Chicago

COPYWRITER | Jay Dandy

CLIENT | Heitman Retail Properties

TOOLS | Adobe Photoshop and Illustrator, Macintosh

DESIGN FIRM | Jeff Fisher Logo Motives
CREATIVE DIRECTOR | Sara Perrin, Seattle Seahawks
DESIGNER/ILLUSTRATOR | Jeff Fisher
PHOTOGRAPHERS | Various
COPYWRITER | Sara Perrin
CLIENT | Seattle Seahawks
TOOLS | Macromedia FreeHand, Macintosh
PRINTING PROCESS | Six-color process

This multi-element package of materials for the Seattle
Seahawks promotes their 1998–1999 season. Various
pieces can be used to target potential corporate sponsors,
season-ticket holders, and the general public.

東亞興業有限公司
EAST ASIA HELLER LIMITED

DESIGN FIRM | Alan Chan Design Company
ART DIRECTOR | Alan Chan
DESIGNERS | Alan Chan, Jiao Ping
CLIENT | East Asia Heller Ltd.

The fish visual was adopted to symbolize the proficient and Chinese-focused services the client provides. Four Chinese idioms, each containing a word-play on fish, were used to highlight four successful business stories. The cover is a familiar Chinese-style dish with an acetate overlay of a fish; this layout allows the fish to transfer over the empty plate—a metaphor for prosperity and abundance.

如魚得水

東亞興萊勇於打破傳統的融資方式，為高雅線圈提供發票貼現與機器租賃服務；信貸額緊隨銷售額遞增，緊密配合高雅線圈急速擴展的業務，令公司業務架構日益完備。從無至有，有賴融資及時而充足，如魚得水。

Who Is UIS?

DESIGN FIRM | **Tom Fowler, Inc.**
ART DIRECTOR | **Thomas G. Fowler**
DESIGNER | **Karl S. Maruyama**
PHOTOGRAPHER | **Tod Bryant/Shooter, Inc.**
COPYWRITER | **Brad Elliot**
CLIENT | **UIS, Inc.**
TOOLS | **QuarkXPress, Adobe Illustrator and Photoshop**
PAPER | **Neenah Classic Columns, Zanders Ikono Gloss**
PRINTING PROCESS | **Offset and foil stamping**

UIS needed a brochure to send to brokers and prospective sellers describing who they are, what kind of business they buy, and the kinds of products their subsidiaries produce.

U I S

Dom Antonellis joined New England Confectionery as an engineer. His first assignment: Modernize the company's outdated production lines. That success led to others, and in 1978 he became president, a position he holds today. "We've built an organization in which companies can thrive" he says. "There is no corporate bureaucracy to deal with, and by bringing so many great brands together we open the way to more effective marketing and stronger year-round sales."

More than eight billion Sweetheart Conversation Hearts are sold annually, and together with NECCO's Sweet Talk line they make the company the leading manufacturer of these products. Contempo-rary slogans keep this classic brand fresh and product popularity high.

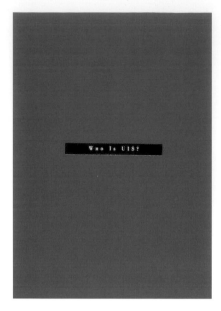

Masterpieces is an extension of the famous Candy Cupboard line of boxed chocolates. Marketed exclusively through more than 2,000 K-Mart stores across the country, the brand was created to further strengthen the entire company's position in the mass merchandiser marketplace.

U I S

First produced in 1847, Necco Wafers is the company's best-selling item and among the top 10 U.S. brands in its category. The candy's popularity continues to grow, providing a strong centerpiece for the marketing of many of the company's other lines and brands.

Confectionery

The New England Confectionery Company is the oldest multi-line candy company in the United States. UIS acquired it in 1963. Today, with its two divisions, Stark Candy Company and Haviland Candy, Company, the $100-million company is steadily expanding through a highly aggressive brand development strategy, year-round product marketing programs and strategic acquisitions.

Haviland Thin Mints became the top-selling brand in its category after UIS acquired the company. Today it is one of the backbones of the company's comprehensive product line.

Mary Janes was primarily a regional brand of molasses taffy when UIS acquired its manufacturer, the Stark Candy Company, in 1990. Over the next six years, sales increased by a factor of 375 as the original brand expanded into a line of its own featuring both everyday and seasonal items.

PAGE 7

every day in America **8** firefighters
will suffer a respiratory injury.
of those, **1** out of **24** will die.

over **56,000** deaths and injuries
were related to Carbon Monoxide
over a period of **10** years.
no other poisonous agent has
ever been implicated in
so many deaths.

about 250 people die,

and thousands more are injured each year from accidental Carbon Monoxide poisoning.

On a Tuesday, in one of our plants that is environmentally controlled, with stringent, comprehensive Electrostatic Discharge (ESD) systems in place, where Die Attachment, Calibration, Wire Bonding and highly sensitive, proprietary operations are performed in a class 1000 clean room - hazardous gas detection equipment is manufactured by hand specifically for, among others, the challenging tasks of today's Firefighter.

At the same time dashing from a hazardous response truck, a Firefighter responds to the urgent need to assess the threat of a grimy railcar-derailment, spilling Chlorine gas, or perhaps to a lethal domestic Carbon Monoxide leak from a household furnace some half a hemisphere away. In an instant, two worlds meet over a gas-safety device which in either case will serve to protect and save human life - an AIM Safety gas detector.

AIM Safety gas detection products have always brought people and safety together. The relationships we've formed over gas safety are significant and deep. Friendships with our nations fire departments... with industrial corporations, utilities and select marketing partners... with our customers and within communities - these are the relationships that help define us as a company, set us apart, and are responsible for our growth and success.

DESIGN FIRM | Big Eye Creative, Inc.

ART DIRECTOR/DESIGNER | Perry Chua

ILLUSTRATOR | Stephen Dittberner

PHOTOGRAPHERS | Grant Waddell, Dann Ilicic

COPYWRITER | Craig Holm

CLIENT | Aim Safety Company, Inc.

TOOLS | Adobe Illustrator and Photoshop, QuarkXPress

PAPER | Cover and text: Utopia;
financial section: Potlatch Karma Natural

PRINTING PROCESS | Six colors: four process, spot metallic,
spot varnish

The watering can is a universal symbol of careful nurturing, growth, and rejuvenation of life, and here it represents the seeds of the future carefully planted by management. The concept also relates nicely with Aim's main business—saving lives with their gas-detection equipment.

Customer Care Anywhere

To succeed in today's communications market, you need to find ways to provide customer service that will set you apart from the competition. And you need to control the steadily increas...

you de...

cost eff...

The A...

The in...

reduce...

decreas...

gather...

more...

To-ass...

develop...

custome...

and bil...

Systems That Wo...

AMS has developed a family of software platforms for communications co...

the entire customer care and billing cycle - from turnkey systems for...

service to subsystems for specific functions such as real time ra...

and credit risk management. Our platforms can be inte...

operating environment and customized to meet sp...

echnology and provides the maxim...

InvoiceConnect

In the competitive telecommunications marketplace, service is a critical factor in customer retention. This is especially true with your important commercial accounts. Improving the value of your billing services can be a key to retaining their business.

InvoiceConnect™, part of AMS's Tapestry™ suite of customer care and billing solutions, offers you a unique way to enhance your customer service. With InvoiceConnect, consolidated usage information from one or multiple billing streams and bill analysis tools is delivered to customers on CD-ROM or via the Internet. This self installing Windows-based application provides a single platform from which business customers can allocate costs, export data, see cost trends and investigate abuse or fraud.

InvoiceConnect gives your customers a powerful interactive system that can streamline the way they manage their communications expenses. And it gives you a way to provide the level of billing service that your corporate accounts demand.

TAPESTRY

1 9 9 6

ANNUAL REPORT

Linn Area Credit Union

DESIGN FIRM | Marketing & Communication Strategies Inc.

DESIGNER | Lloyd Keels

PHOTOGRAPHER | Marketing & Communication Strategies Inc.

CLIENT | Linn Area Credit Union

TOOLS | QuarkXPress, Adobe Illustrator and Photoshop

PAPER | Neenah Classic Laid cover; Olympian 80 lb. coated text

PRINTING PROCESS | Two color offset

The client wished to have an annual report that was modern and classy without a lot of printing extras. A two-color design with ornate icons and interesting page headers and footers created a piece that conveyed the personality of the growing credit union.

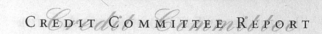

AUDIT COMMITTEE REPORT

The Audit Committee is responsible for monitoring and evaluating credit union activities. The committee reviews credit union procedures to ensure that the highest degree of integrity is maintained in operations and that the Credit Union adheres to all federal and state laws and regulations.

This year, the Audit Committee retained the auditing firm of Petersen & Associates of Omaha, Nebraska, to assist in carrying out its responsibilities. This firm conducted a comprehensive audit and performed a full examination of the Credit Union's financial statements for the calendar year 1996. The audit and examination revealed no areas of concern and confirmed the soundness of the Credit Union. A letter from the firm's latest audit is included in this report.

Each year, Petersen & Associates performs a verification of member account balances and requests that members notify them of any discrepancies. No significant discrepancies have been reported. The Audit Committee also works with the firm to evaluate the internal controls that are used in the operation of the Credit Union to be sure that all areas of risk are adequately controlled.

In addition to this independent assessment, our Internal Auditor randomly monitors operations through a continuous program of random loan reviews, member account verifications, and other audit procedures to ensure the safety and soundness of your credit union.

Linn Area Credit Union is also examined, on an annual basis, by the Credit Union Division of the State of Iowa. This examination assessed the Credit Union's lending practices and financial operations for compliance with applicable laws and regulations. Linn Area Credit Union was given a favorable report.

As a result of the independent audits, examinations and the observations of the committee, it is our belief that the enclosed financial statements fairly and accurately reflect the financial condition of Linn Area Credit Union as of December 31, 1996.

DONALD WARREN
AUDIT COMMITTEE CHAIRMAN

LLOYD BAIRD

VERYL SIEVERS

CREDIT COMMITTEE REPORT

RAY VANDERWIEL
CREDIT COMMITTEE CHAIRMAN

KENT BAKER

R. MICHAEL GILLEN

The Credit Committee establishes guidelines for the Credit Union's lending programs. The committee has empowered a staff of professional loan officers to meet the borrowing needs of our members and provide knowledgeable solutions and advice. Members are offered a wide range of personal and real estate loans at competitive rates and terms.

Loan demand continued to be active in 1996. Loans granted to members increased 17.3% over the prior year. The Credit Committee is especially pleased to report that the quality of the loan portfolio is outstanding. Throughout the year we maintained very minimal delinquency. At year end only 17 credit cards totaling $57,499.68 were delinquent, and just 7 consumer loans for $47,019.54 and one $195,653.88 mortgage were past due more than 60 days. Out of 5,690 loans this is an incredibly low number and reflects the high moral standards of our members and the fine work of our lending staff.

The mortgage department was busy with first mortgage, construction loan, and refinancing activity throughout the year due to rates maintaining historically low levels. Credit Union members were granted 220 first mortgage loans totaling $16.8 million. This included 23 construction loans, a 69% increase over the prior year. With projections that the current interest rate environment will remain steady, it looks like 1997 will be a very active year as well.

Our MASTERCARD, VISA Classic and VISA Gold programs continue to increase in numbers and attract new members. With all three cards at very competitive interest rates and terms, we were able to increase credit card outstandings to $4,917,817, up from $3,968,248 in December of 1995. The total number of cards has increased from 2,723 to 3,150 reflecting the favorable rates that the Credit Union has to offer.

We congratulate and thank our loan staff for their exceptional efforts over the past year. We also thank you for utilizing the Credit Union for all of your borrowing needs and we look forward to serving you in the future.

DESIGN FIRM | Belyea Design Alliance

ART DIRECTOR | Patricia Belyea

DESIGNER | Ron Lars Hansen

PHOTOGRAPHER | Jim Linna

COPYWRITER | Toby Todd

CLIENT | Pacific Market International

PAPER | Strobe, Classic Columns

PRINTING PROCESS | Hexachrome

This brochure gives an overview of PMI's philosophy, capabilities, and services. The bold product shots are designed to show the company's focus on detail and the active-lifestyle market they target.

1997 ANNUAL REPORT

Last year, we made a commitment to grow.

United Concordia Companies™

DESIGN FIRM | BrabenderCox
ART DIRECTOR/DESIGNER | Kevin Rayman
PHOTOGRAPHER | Stock, Pat Leeson
COPYWRITERS | Kevin Rayman, Sarah Starr
CLIENT | United Concordia
TOOLS | QuarkXPress, Adobe Illustrator and Photoshop
PAPER | Fox River Sundance, Strathmore Elements
PRINTING PROCESS | Black plus PMS Warm Gray, duotone photos

The client wanted to relate their success in the past year along with a down-to-earth feeling. Because of the small amount of information used in this piece, the designers felt it was important to let the delivery of the information communicate its importance, thus the fold-out pocket folder with inserts.

DESIGN FIRM | Ramona Hutko Design
ALL DESIGN | Ramona Hutko
CLIENT | Computer Sciences Corporation
TOOLS | Adobe Illustrator, QuarkXPress, Macintosh
PAPER | Mohawk Superfine
PRINTING PROCESS | Offset

Since the building interior was incomplete, type was used as illustration depicting the main messages

Executive Briefing Center

Computer Sciences Corporation

CSC

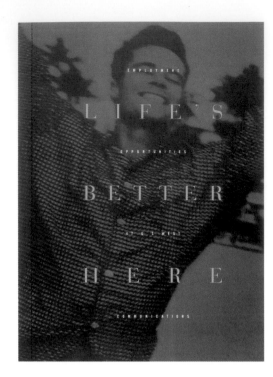

DESIGN FIRM | Vaughn Wedeen Creative
ART DIRECTOR | Steve Wedeen
COPYWRITER | Foster Hurley
CLIENT | US West

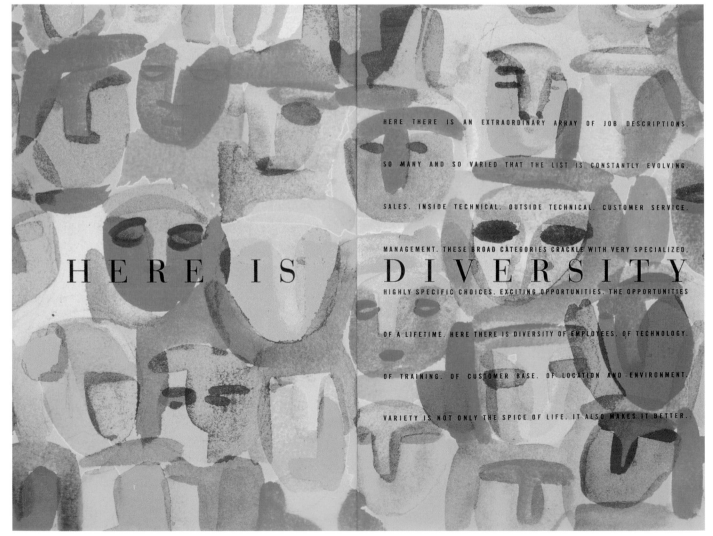

HERE IS DIVERSITY

HERE THERE IS AN EXTRAORDINARY ARRAY OF JOB DESCRIPTIONS.

SO MANY AND SO VARIED THAT THE LIST IS CONSTANTLY EVOLVING.

SALES. INSIDE TECHNICAL. OUTSIDE TECHNICAL. CUSTOMER SERVICE.

MANAGEMENT. THESE BROAD CATEGORIES CRACKLE WITH VERY SPECIALIZED,

HIGHLY SPECIFIC CHOICES. EXCITING OPPORTUNITIES. THE OPPORTUNITIES

OF A LIFETIME. HERE THERE IS DIVERSITY OF EMPLOYEES. OF TECHNOLOGY.

OF TRAINING. OF CUSTOMER BASE. OF LOCATION AND ENVIRONMENT.

VARIETY IS NOT ONLY THE SPICE OF LIFE. IT ALSO MAKES IT BETTER.

DESIGN FIRM | Insight Design Communications

ART DIRECTORS/DESIGNERS | Tracy and Sherrie Holdeman

CLIENT | Solid Solutions

TOOLS | Macromedia FreeHand

By emphasizing the actual recycling efforts of the company, the designers chose a practical way to illustrate the company mission.

DESIGN FIRM | The Riordon Design Group, Inc.

ART DIRECTOR | Ric Riordon

DESIGNERS | Dan Wheaton, Shirley Riordon, Greer Hutchison, Sharon Pece

PHOTOGRAPHER | Robert Lear

COPYWRITERS | Shirley Riordon, Dan Wheaton, Greer Hutchison

CLIENT | JJM Manufacturing

TOOLS | QuarkXPress, Adobe Photoshop and Illustrator

PAPER | Supreme Gloss Cover, Glama Vellum

PRINTING PROCESS | Four-color stochastic (Somerset Graphics)

Inspired by the client's commission to create a public-relations piece specifically aimed at the high-end corporate market, the designers used soft, textural images and natural colors to visually imply the qualities of the sportswear.

GOLF • The JJM Tour Line goes the distance with soft, 100% cotton lightweight fabrics, subtle patterns and rich hues. The Tour Line embodies a refined style and easy comfort that won't leave you in the rough.

the art of looking good.

It's all about style and quality – it's about being noticed. We're in the business of dressing up your corporate image. More specifically, we design, manufacture and customize garments for companies worldwide.

Our garments are created with careful attention to the smallest detail. Choose from a discerning two-button placket or make a statement with a stylish zippered closure. Our golf shirts will bring you in under par, with labels strategically placed on the right sleeve, to help prevent hooks or slices.

DESIGN FIRM | Sound Transit
ART DIRECTOR/DESIGNER | Anthony Secolo
COPYWRITER | Evelyn Eldridge, Tim Healy
CLIENT | Sound Transit
TOOLS | Adobe PageMaker, Macromedia FreeHand
PAPER | Matrix Coronado
PRINTING PROCESS | Two-color plus varnish

Successful elements include metallic ink for the image in metallic monotone and the radius diecut. The client response to this report was ecstatic.

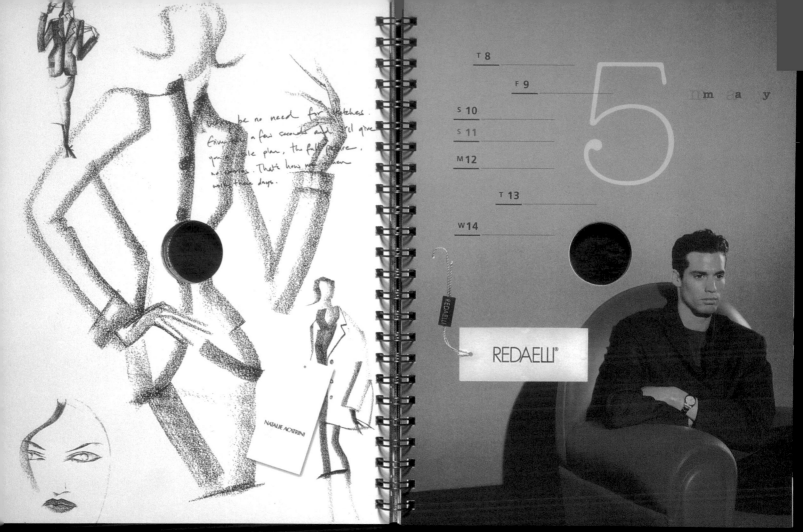

DESIGN FIRM | Alan Chan Design Company
ART DIRECTOR | Alan Chan
DESIGNERS | Alan Chan, Miu Choy, Pamela Low
COPYWRITER | Lam Ping Ting
CLIENT | Swank Shop

The spring/summer fashion catalogue portrays the
evolutionary process of Hong Kong and its fashion scene
during rule by the British. The legend of Nu Wo repairing
the hole in the sky is also included in the design.

DESIGN FIRM | Mervil Paylor Design

ART DIRECTOR/DESIGNER | Mervil M. Paylor

PHOTOGRAPHER | Stock, Kelly Culpepper

COPYWRITER | Melissa Stone

CLIENT | The Close Family

TOOLS | Adobe Photoshop and PageMaker

PAPER | Strathmore Grande

The client is the majority stockholder in Springs Industries, manufacturer of select Ultrasuede.® The branch attached to the cover comes from one of the 6,000 Fort Mill, South Carolina, peach trees grown by client's family since the mid-1800s.

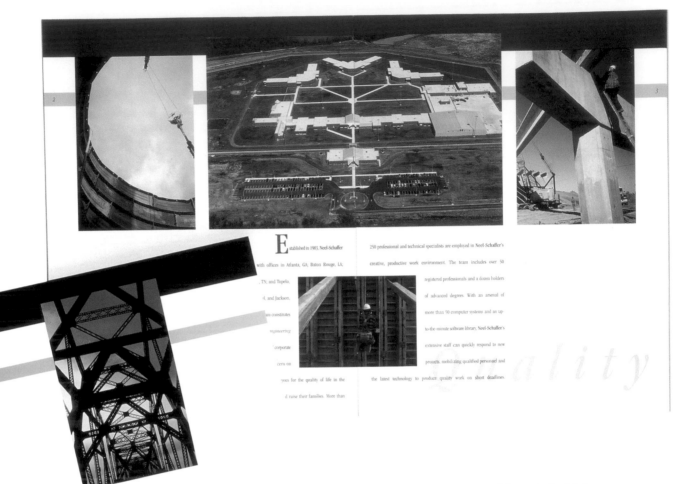

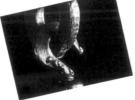

NEEL-SCHAFFER, INC.
ENGINEERS · PLANNERS · LANDSCAPE ARCHITECTS

DESIGN FIRM | Communication Arts Company

ART DIRECTOR | Hap Owen

DESIGNER | Anne-Marie Otvos Cain

COPYWRITER | David Adcock

CLIENT | Neel-Schaffer, Inc.

TOOLS | Macromedia FreeHand, Adobe Photoshop

PAPER | Potlatch Karma, Neenah classic laid, Kromekote

PRINTING PROCESS | Five-color, offset lithography

The purpose of this booklet was to highlight the client's vast capabilities. Their large-scale projects called for large-scale photographs. The challenge was to keep rhythm and symmetry throughout using a variety of photographs and subjects.

MONTREAL
SEGURANÇA E VIGILÂNCIA

DESIGN FIRM | AWG Graphics Communicação, Ltda.
ART DIRECTOR | Renata Claudia de Cristofaro
DESIGNER | Luciana Vieira
PHOTOGRAPHER | Fabio Rubinato
CLIENT | Montreal Segurança
TOOLS | Adobe Photoshop, CorelDraw, PC
PAPER | Couchê 150 gsm
PRINTING PROCESS | Offset

The creative concept shows the company and its employees right on the cover, so prospective clients will see immediately what Montreal services deliver. The fusion of images reinforces the creative concept.

DESIGN FIRM | The Creative Response Company, Inc.

ART DIRECTOR/DESIGNERS | Creative Team

COPYWRITERS | Creative Copy Team

CLIENT | Sun City Marketing

TOOLS | Adobe Photoshop and PageMaker,
Macromedia FreeHand

PRINTING PROCESS | Offset

The objective of this brochure was to position
Buckingham Palace as a first-class residential
condominium, fit for a king with the most
discriminating taste. To achieve this objective, the
creative team used an oversized trim, cut with
elegant fonts and handsome photos printed on
special paper to emphasize grandeur. A hard-bound
cover was used with foil stamping to complete the
nobility image the client desired.

DESIGN FIRM | Melissa Passehl Design
ART DIRECTOR | Melissa Passehl
DESIGNERS | Melissa Passehl, Charlotte Lambrechts
PROJECT MANAGER/WRITER | Caroline Ocampo
PHOTOGRAPHER | Geoffrey Nelson
COPYWRITER | Susan Sharpe
CLIENT | Girls Scouts Annual Report 1995–1996: Girl Power
TOOLS | QuarkXPress, Adobe Illustrator and Photoshop
PAPER | Gilclear and Lustro Gloss
PRINTING PROCESS | Two-color lithography

This annual report defines girl power as it relates
to a day-in-the-life of a Girl Scout. The designers used
a tall, thin format with bold type, graphic color, and a
photojournalistic approach to show how Girl Scouts
promote programs that enable the development of
character, courage, respect, honor, strength, and wisdom.

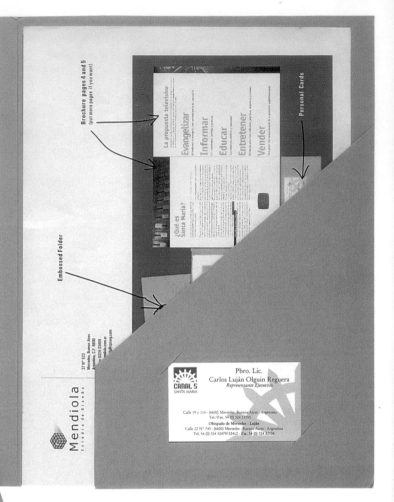

DESIGN FIRM | Mendiola Design Studio

ART DIRECTOR | Matias Mendiola

DESIGNER | Rafael Munarriz

PHOTOGRAPHER | Mendiola Design Studio

COPYWRITERS | Natalia Marchetti, Santa Maria Channel

CLIENT | Santa Maria Channel (television)

TOOLS | CorelDraw, Adobe PageMaker and Photoshop

PAPER | Witcel S.A.

PRINTING PROCESS | Four-color offset, embossed

The beautifully embossed folder serves two functions:
It maintains the brochure safely and stores other
important documents with the brochure.

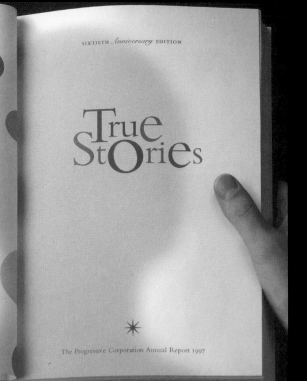

SIXTIETH *Anniversary* EDITION

True StOries

✳

The Progressive Corporation Annual Report 1997

DESIGN FIRM | Nesnadny & Schwartz

ART DIRECTORS | Mark Schwartz, Joyce Nesnadny

DESIGNERS | Joyce Nesnadny, Michelle Moehler

PHOTOGRAPHERS | Ron Baxter Smith, cover;
Design Photography, artwork

COPYWRITER | Peter B. Lewis, The Progressive Corporation

CLIENT | The Progressive Corporation

TOOLS | Trade Gothic, QuarkXPress

PAPER | French Construction Whitewash 100 lb. cover;
French Parchtone White 60 lb. text, uncoated fly;
SD Warren Strobe Gloss 100 lb. coated text;
French Frostone Flurry 70 lb. uncoated text

PRINTING PROCESS | Outside cover: four-color process plus dull
aqueous coating; inside cover: three match
colors plus dull aqueous coating;
five special match colors, uncoated fly;
four-color process plus gloss varnish,
coated text; six special match colors,
uncoated text

In a free-association test recently administered to 1,153 college students, the word "insurance" prompted the response "romance" in 82.8% of cases...Alright, we admit it—we're only kidding. Still, for our claim representatives (at our more than 350 claim offices), romance isn't an unknown continent. On a recent Saturday evening, Chandra Haines, a Progressive claim representative in Savannah, Georgia came to the rescue of a young couple involved in a fender bender. She helped them contact their families, and, despite the late hour, arranged to have their car repaired immediately. The couple, who had just been married, were heading to Florida for their honeymoon and had thought for certain their trip was ruined. But they weren't counting on the efficiency of Progressive's Immediate Response® claims service. In a romantic cause, our claim representatives stand ready to slay any dragon.

the
rOmance
of
immediate respOnse

no. 4

Marty Ackley, mixed media on canvas, 1997

12

DESIGN FIRM | Hornall Anderson Design Works, Inc.

ART DIRECTOR | Jack Anderson

DESIGNERS | Jack Anderson, Lisa Cerveny, Heidi Favour,
Jana Wilson Esser

ILLUSTRATOR | Hornall Anderson Design Works, Inc.

PHOTOGRAPHER | Tom Collicott

COPYWRITER | Scott Ford

CLIENT | Novell, Inc.

TOOLS | QuarkXPress

PAPER | Signature dull, UV Ultra

This corporate profile displays the company's vast
networking experience. It was important to create
a brochure that emphasized business-to-business
communication, and had a straightforward, easy-
to-read approach to its technical information.

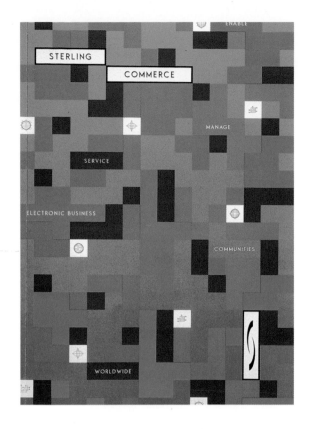

DESIGN FIRM | Pinkhaus Design

ART DIRECTOR | Kristin Johnson

DESIGNER/ILLUSTRATOR | Raelene Mercer

PHOTOGRAPHER | John Running

COPYWRITER | Frank Cunningham

CLIENT | Sterling Commerce

TOOLS | QuarkXPress, Adobe Illustrator and Photoshop

PAPER | Potlatch McCoy Velour

PRINTING PROCESS | Offset 8/8, four-color process plus two Pantone plus two varnishes (dull and gloss)

Sterling requested their story be told through the voice of their customers. The creative inspiration was driven by the graphic image the designers established for Sterling Commerce during this past year.

Nobody can tell our story better than our clients. We asked twelve of them, each representative of a different industry, to share their experience. The fact is, we have 40,000 other clients, each with a similar story to tell. But that's a bigger brochure than we wanted to tackle.

ASK

AND THEY'LL TELL YOU

10

11

DESIGN FIRM | The Leonhardt Group
DESIGNERS | Greg Morgan, Janee Kreinheder
ILLUSTRATOR | Greg Morgan
PHOTOGRAPHER | Europe: John Rees; shoes:Don Mason
COPYWRITER | Renee Sullivan, Jodi Eschom
CLIENT | Nordstrom
PAPER | Cougar Opaque

Nordstrom wanted their shoe catalog to go beyond
the traditional, to be artistic and tactile, yet maintain the feel and look of Nordstrom. The message is
conveyed by the your-feet-take-you-places theme,
while the designed-in-Europe message is subtly
expressed by the destination imagery and exotic
foreign postage stamps.

NORDSTROM

opposite and this page, D: **Nordstrom 'Dayton'** sandal. When it comes to comfort, this is a global
classic. Camel, red or black: **59.95**. E: **Nordstrom 'Darcy'** loafer. As easy as a lazy gondola ride.
Beige or black: **59.95**. Both styles feature an unlined nubuck upper and latex rubber sole. In sizes
7-11n, 4-12,13m, 6-10w. In Women's Shoes

page six

page seven

DESIGN FIRM | Michael Courtney Design

ART DIRECTOR | Michael Courtney

DESIGNERS | Michael Courtney, Michelle Rieb, Bill Strong

PHOTOGRAPHER | Pete Eckert, Eckert & Eckert

COPYWRITER | Leslie Brown, In Other Words

CLIENT | Mahlum Architects

TOOLS | Adobe PageMaker and Photoshop

Mahlum wanted to create a one-of-a-kind invitation
that would draw past, current, and prospective
clients to their new office space, and that could be
used also for their long-term marketing objectives.

DESIGN FIRM | Hornall Anderson Design Works, Inc.

ART DIRECTORS | John Hornall, Lisa Cerveny

DESIGNERS | John Hornall, Lisa Cerveny, Heidi Favour,
Bruce Branson-Meyer

PHOTOGRAPHER | Robin Bartholick

COPYWRITER | Elaine Floyd

CLIENT | Airborne Express

TOOLS | QuarkXPress, Macromedia FreeHand, Adobe Photoshop

PAPER | Mohawk Superfine

Large, bold type and photographic images stress the
company's inherent goals: acceleration, frequency,
momentum, consistency, and potential. Each photo reflects
movement, which emphasizes the client's business of
swift international air-courier services.

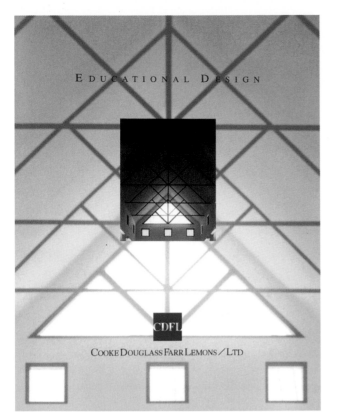

EDUCATIONAL DESIGN

CDFL

COOKE DOUGLASS FARR LEMONS / LTD

DESIGN FIRM | Communication Arts Company

ART DIRECTOR | Hilda Stauss Owen

DESIGNER | Anne-Marie Otvos Cain

COPYWRITER | David Adcock

CLIENT | Cooke Douglass Farr Lemons, Ltd.

TOOLS | Macromedia FreeHand, Adobe Photoshop

PAPER | Patina matte

PRINTING PROCESS | 5/5, offset lithography

The second in a series of booklets, this piece focuses on the firm's educational design work. Although the booklets had to be produced at three different points during the year, they were designed simultaneously to keep the look consistent throughout the series.

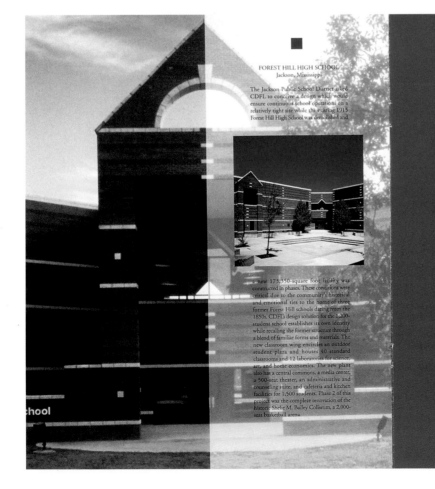

FOREST HILL HIGH SCHOOL
Jackson, Mississippi

The Jackson Public School District asked CDFL to conceive a design which would ensure continuous school operations on a relatively tight site while the existing 1915 Forest Hill High School was demolished and a new 173,350-square foot facility was constructed in phases. These conditions were critical due to the community's historical and emotional ties to the home of three former Forest Hill schools dating from the 1850s. CDFL's design solution for the 1,200-student school establishes its own identity while recalling the former structure through a blend of familiar forms and materials. The new classroom wing encircles an outdoor student plaza and houses 40 standard classrooms and 12 laboratories for science, art, and home economics. The new plant also has a central commons, a media center, a 500-seat theater, an administrative and counseling suite, and cafeteria and kitchen facilities for 1,500 students. Phase 2 of this project was the complete renovation of the historic Shelie M. Bailey Coliseum, a 2,000-seat basketball arena.

CDFL Selected Clients:

HIGHER EDUCATION
Alcorn State University
Auburn University
Baylor University
Belhaven College
Hinds Community College
Indiana State University
Jackson State University
Mississippi State University
Mississippi University for Women
University of Arkansas
University of Mississippi
University of Mississippi Medical Center

PUBLIC & PRIVATE
SCHOOL SYSTEMS
Claiborne County School District
Clinton Public School District
First Presbyterian Day School
Hazlehurst Public School District
Hillcrest Christian School
Hinds County Public Schools
Jackson Public School District
Jackson Preparatory School
Montgomery County School District
Quitman County School District
Rankin County School District
Pearl Public School District
Sharkey-Issaquena Line
Consolidated School District
Simpson County School District
Winona Public School District
Vicksburg-Warren School District

GOVERNMENTAL
Mississippi Bureau of Buildings
Mississippi Department of Education
United States Department of Labor

I DON'T PERSONALLY KNOW
MOST OF THE PEOPLE WHO
HAVE EVER LISTENED TO MY
MUSIC. BUT JUST BECAUSE
I DON'T KNOW THEIR NAMES
DOESN'T MEAN I'M NOT
CONNECTED TO THEM IN SOME WAY.

Music has the power to connect us — to a feeling, to ourselves, to each other, to God, to what we believe.

DESIGN FIRM | Anderson Thomas Design, Inc.
ART DIRECTOR/DESIGNER | Susan Browne
ILLUSTRATOR | Kristi Carter (hand lettering)
PHOTOGRAPHERS | Kurt Markus, Just Loomis
COPYWRITER | Amy Grant
CLIENT | Amy Grant Productions/Blanton Harrell
       Entertainment
TOOLS | QuarkXPress, Adobe Photoshop
PAPER | Gilbert Voice, Sandpiper, Warren Lustro Dull
PRINTING PROCESS | Four-color process plus dry-trap
       gloss plus dull varnishes

The client requested a clean, understated,
sophisticated design, specifically not Photoshop
layered. The album title lent itself to the image of
Amy Grant looking directly at the camera; the design
unfolded aournd this. There was a tight deadline
for this project; after photography, the concept and
design/engraving/printing were completed in about
four weeks.

DESIGN FIRM | Sayles Graphic Design

ALL DESIGN | John Sayles

PHOTOGRAPHER | Bill Nellans

COPYWRITER | Jill Schroeder

CLIENT | BCS Insurance Company

PAPER | Terracoat cream

PRINTING PROCESS | Offset

Targeted to BCS affiliates with investment interests, the announcement arrives in an elegant presentation box. The hinged lid is printed with a pattern of illustrations: bulls, bears, and currency symbols printed in copper, silver, and gold metallic inks on a marbled paper stock. Inside, a fitted tray holds a brochure filled with dramatic four-color photo collages, bold illustrations, and copy printed on alternating cast-coated and marbleized pages, along with a special gift: a glass paperweight etched with a bull.

DESIGN FIRM | Vardimon Design
ART DIRECTOR | Yarom Vardimon
DESIGNERS | Yarom Vardimon, D. Goldberg, G. Ron
PHOTOGRAPHER | Avi Ganor
COPYWRITER | Copirite Y. Fachler
CLIENT | Elite Industries Ltd.
PRINTING PROCESS | Offset

The photographer tried to show the cut-outs imaginatively, in three dimensions, to emphasize the company's A-brands.

SₙAₐLTᴄKᵧYₛ

TAKING THE MARKET BY STORM

IN JUST 5 YEARS, ELITE HAS ACHIEVED A DOMINANT SHARE OF THE SALTY SNACK MARKET, VASTLY INCREASING TOTAL SALES VOLUME IN THIS EXPANDING MARKET. ELITE NOW ACCOUNTS FOR MORE THAN 50% OF THE POTATO CHIP MARKET AND 25% OF THE PUFFED CORN SNACKS MARKET.

UNDER A LICENSING AGREEMENT WITH "FRITO-LAY", PART OF "PEPSICO FOODS INTERNATIONAL", ELITE PRODUCES "RUFFLES", THE WORLD'S NUMBER ONE POTATO CHIP SNACK; "CHEETOS", THE POPULAR CHEESE-FLAVORED SNACK; AND "DORITOS", THE CORN CHIPS FAVORITE. OTHER LOCALLY DEVELOPED AND MANUFACTURED PRODUCTS SUCH AS "SHOOSH" ARE WELL ESTABLISHED IN THE DOMESTIC MARKET, AND ENJOYED BY A WIDE CROSS-SECTION OF THE CONSUMER PUBLIC.

ELITE'S ENTRY INTO THE SALTY SNACK MARKET HAS PROVED A RESOUNDING SUCCESS. THE WIDE VARIETY OF DIFFERENT PRODUCTS NOW AVAILABLE HAS INCREASED DEMAND AND RAISED THE QUALITY OF SNACKS ON THE MARKET BY OFFERING HEALTHY AND VITAMIN-ENRICHED PRODUCTS WITH WIDE CONSUMER APPEAL.

WITHIN 5 YEARS OF ENTERING THE MARKET, ELITE ACHIEVED A DOMINANT SHARE OF THE SALTY SNACK MARKET. DORITOS (THE CORN CHIPS WITH THE LOUDEST TASTE ON EARTH), HAVE ALREADY BECOME A FIRM FAVORITE.

DESIGN FIRM | Pepe Gimeno, S.L.

DESIGNER | Pepe Gimeno

CLIENT | Feria Internacional del Mueble de Valencia

TOOLS | Macromedia FreeHand, Adobe Photoshop

General Motors
Pontiac GMC Division

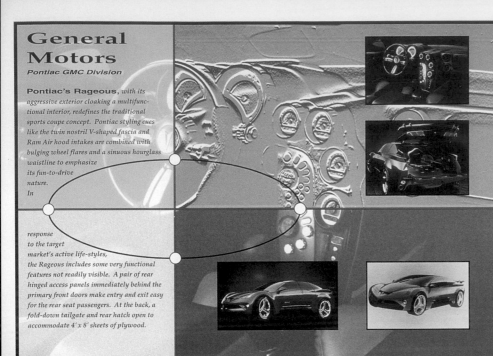

Pontiac's Rageous, *with its aggressive exterior cloaking a multifunctional interior, redefines the traditional sports coupe concept. Pontiac styling cues like the twin nostril V-shaped fascia and Ram Air hood intakes are combined with bulging wheel flares and a sinuous hourglass waistline to emphasize its fun-to-drive nature. In*

response to the target market's active life-styles, the Rageous includes some very functional features not readily visible. A pair of rear hinged access panels immediately behind the primary front doors make entry and exit easy for the rear seat passengers. At the back, a fold-down tailgate and rear hatch open to accommodate 4' x 8' sheets of plywood.

ALL DESIGN | Barry Hutzel
COPYWRITER | Roger Quinlan
CLIENT | IDSA Michigan Chapter
TOOLS | Adobe PageMaker and Photoshop
PAPER | Neenah Classic Columns 80 lb. cover;
       Romaine #1 house stock gloss 80 lb. text
PRINTING PROCESS | Two color

This yearly publication is a showcase for Michigan Industrial Designers' products. The budget was kept down by producing a two-color piece that took full advantage of the colored cover stock.

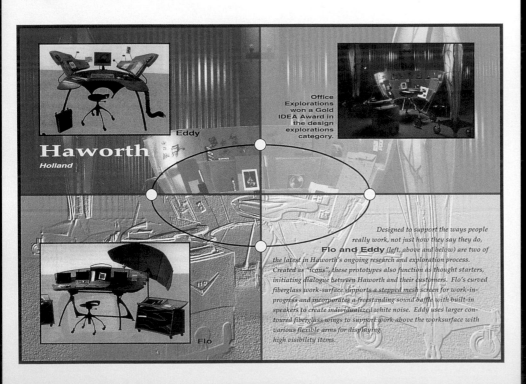

Eddy

Haworth
Holland

Office Explorations won a Gold IDEA Award in the design explorations category.

Designed to support the ways people really work, not just how they say they do, **Flo and Eddy** *(left, above and below) are two of the latest in Haworth's ongoing research and exploration process. Created as "icons", these prototypes also function as thought starters, initiating dialogue between Haworth and their customers. Flo's curved fiberglass work-surface supports a stepped mesh screen for work-in-progress and incorporates a freestanding sound baffle with built-in speakers to create individualized white noise. Eddy uses larger contoured fiberglass wings to support work above the worksurface with various flexible arms for displaying high visibility items.*

Flo

DESIGN FIRM | Goodhue & Associés Design Communication
CREATIVE DIRECTOR | Lise Charbonneau
ART DIRECTOR | Paulo Correia
DESIGNERS | Josée Barsalo, Dany DeGrâce
ILLUSTRATOR | Caroline Merola
PHOTOGRAPHER | Jean Vachon
COPYWRITER | Ivanhoe, Communications and Public Affairs
CLIENT | Ivanhoe Inc.
TOOLS | QuarkXPress, Macromedia FreeHand,
Adobe Photoshop
PRINTING PROCESS | Offset

The client, a real-estate giant specializing in shopping centers, sought to show prospective investors its sound expertise and flair for innovation. Outsized images and classical serif type draw the reader in.

STRENGTH

IVANHOE IS WITHOUT DOUBT A FORCE
IN THE CANADIAN REAL ESTATE INDUSTRY

Ivanhoe is one of Canada's most respected property management, development and investment companies, specializing in quality shopping centers in urban areas. ■ As soon as the Company appeared on the scene early in the 1950s, it began carving out a place for itself in the real estate sector. Today it is active across the country, primarily in Quebec and Ontario, but also in Western Canada through investments in Cambridge. For several years it has been investing in the United States, forming major financial partnerships with a number of U.S. real estate giants. ■ When Ivanhoe was created, it capitalized on the opportunities for rapid growth offered by the marketplace and the economic conditions of the fifties. It was, therefore, well prepared for the economic downturn and the recession of the 1990s and was able to go on investing in a careful and patient manner while continuing to skillfully manage its assets. ■ To meet new challenges, Ivanhoe knows that it can count on dedicated, competent human resources. It has invaluable tools that enable it to adapt to industry change: diversification into foreign markets, strategic alliances, sustained research and development, and a comprehensive marketing program. All these measures are based on a new definition of the shopping center and on the quality of service offered to tenants and consumers. ■ A healthy financial situation and dynamic management of its real estate portfolio and organizational resources have enabled the Company to gradually become a leader. Combining management expertise with solid development and investment capacity, Ivanhoe is without doubt a major force in the real estate industry.

The Company manages a full range of quality shopping centers in Canada and the United States, from neighborhood centers to regional supercenters.

1600 FARADAY AVENUE
CARLSBAD, CA 92008
TELEPHONE: 760-603-7200
FACSIMILE: 760-603-7201
TOLL FREE: 800-955-6288
WWW.INVITROGEN.COM

BOUND PRINTED
MATTER BLK RT
U.S. POSTAGE
PAID
PONTIAC, IL
PERMIT NO. 104

PRODUCT BROCHURES

DESIGN FIRM | Mires Design
ART DIRECTOR | Jose A. Serrano
DESIGNER | Mary Pritchard
ILLUSTRATOR | J. Otto
CLIENT | Invitrogen Corporation
TOOLS | Adobe Illustrator
PAPER | White gloss cover weight
PRINTING PROCESS | Four-color process

The design team created a cover for
this catalog that had a fresh look
without appearing too high tech.

DESIGN FIRM | **McCullough Creative Group, Inc.**

ART DIRECTOR | **Jeff MacFarlane**

DESIGNER | **Jeff MacFarlane**

PHOTOGRAPHERS | **Ken Smith and James Cessna**

COPYWRITER | **Bob Lupinacci**

CLIENT | **Anasazi Exclusive Salon Products, Inc.**

PAPER/PRINTER | **Royal Fiber Natural, Union-Hoermann
    Press**

TOOLS | **QuarkXPress, Macromedia FreeHand,
    and Adobe Photoshop**

The designer chose a 4-color process with a single
spot color.

DESIGN FIRM | Mires Design, Inc.

ART DIRECTOR | Scott Mires

DESIGNER | Scott Mires

PHOTOGRAPHER | Marshall Harrington

CALLIGRAPHER | Judythe Sieck

CLIENT | Taylor Guitars

DESIGN FIRM | The Kuester Group

ART DIRECTOR | Kevin B. Kuester

DESIGNER | Tim Sauer

COPYWRITER | David Forney

CLIENT | Potlatch Corporation, NW Paper Division

PAPER/PRINTER | Vintage Gloss and Velvet, Heritage Press

TOOLS | QuarkXPress, Macromedia FreeHand,
and Adobe Photoshop

1

2

1

DESIGN FIRM | Mires Design, Inc.

ART DIRECTOR | John Ball

DESIGNERS | John Ball and Kathy Carpentier-Moore

ILLUSTRATOR | Gerald Bustamante

CLIENT | California Center For The Arts, Escondido

TOOL | QuarkXPress

This 4-color brochure advertises tickets for the new season.

2

DESIGN FIRM | Hornall Anderson Design Works, Inc.

ART DIRECTOR | Jack Anderson

DESIGNERS | Jack Anderson, David Bates

ILLUSTRATOR | Todd Conno

PHOTOGRAPHER | Darrell Peterson

COPYWRITER | SunDog, Inc.

CLIENT | SunDog, Inc.

PAPER | Recycled Paper

TOOLS | Adobe Photoshop, QuarkXPress, and Macromedia FreeHand

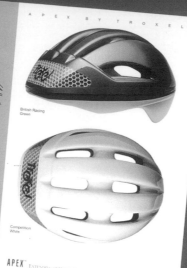

APEX BY TROXEL

British Racing
Green

Competition
White

An integrated visor
shields eyes during long
sunny afternoons and uphill
climbing. Under the visor,
the largest brow vents on
the market draw in cooling
air and make the Apex one
of the best ventilated
helmets available.

THE
ULTIMATE IN
HEAD GEAR,
DESIGNED
EXCLUSIVELY
FOR ROCK
JOCKS AND
OTHER
OFF-ROAD
WARRIORS.

APEX™ EXTENDING OVER THE TEMPLES AND DEEPER IN THE BACK, THE APEX TAKES ITS CUE FROM THE LESSONS LEARNED BY MOTOCROSS RIDERS: IN THE DIRT, ANYTHING IS POSSIBLE. YET THE APEX REMAINS COMPETITIVELY LIGHTWEIGHT AT ONLY 10 OUNCES. ● WITH THE APEX OFF-ROAD HELMET, TROXEL INTRODUCES THE FIRST ENERGY-ABSORBING ALTERNATIVE TO EXPANDED FOAM. SUPRACOR™ IS SUSPENSION-BONDED HONEYCOMB USED WITHIN THE VISOR TO REDUCE WEIGHT AND ENHANCE DURABILITY. THE FEATHERWEIGHT SUPRACOR IS VISIBLE THROUGH THE VISOR WINDOW, AND THE LINER IS MADE OF LIGHTWEIGHT GECET™ FOAM. ● THE APEX ALSO SPORTS FEATURES ONCE A FIERCE PLAYER COULD LIVE EVER SWEAT HUG™ BROW PAD'S UNIQUE OF PERSPIRATION TECHNOLOGY. OUR EXCLUSIVE ABSORBENT MATERIAL WICKS MOISTURE FROM THE FOREHEAD AND TRANSPORTS IT SIDEWAYS, FORCING PERSPIRATION TO DRIP AT THE SIDEBURNS RATHER THAN INTO THE EYES. ● THE INTEGRATED VISOR COMBATS THE GLARING RAYS THAT AFFLICT AFTERNOON ASCENTS. BENEATH THE VISOR, THREE "FLEX-THRU" VENTS CAPTURE THE AIR BEING DEFLECTED FROM THE FOREHEAD AND FORCE IT THROUGH THE CHANNELS. CONSEQUENTLY, COOLER HEADS PREVAIL, EVEN WHEN THEY'RE BURNING THEMSELVES OVER BOULDERS AND THROUGH STICKY BRUSH. ● SNELL B90/ANSI APPROVED. AVAILABLE IN BRITISH RACING GREEN AND COMPETITION WHITE. ADULT SIZES S/M AND L/XL.

DESIGN FIRM | Caldera Design
ART DIRECTORS | Paul Caldera, Doreen Caldera
DESIGNERS | Bart Welch, Tim Fisher
PHOTOGRAPHER | Bob Carey
CLIENT | Troxel Cycling
TOOL | QuarkXPress

Design Firm | Giorgio Rocco Communications
  Design Consultants
Art Director | Giorgio Rocco
Designer | Giorgio Rocco
Photographer | Archives L'Oréal
Copywriter | Anna Andreuzzi
Client | L'Oréal
Paper/Printer | Zanders Matte Paper 167 lb.
Tools | Macromedia FreeHand, and Adobe PageMaker

This presentation kit was printed in 5 colors (4-color process and a single spot color) on matte and transparent papers. We used matt plastification, embossing, and hot gold on the covers. Actress Andie MacDowell provided the testimonial.

DESIGN FIRM | Grafik Communications

ART DIRECTOR | Melanie Bass

DESIGNERS | Melanie Bass, Gregg Glaviano,
and Judy Kirpich

PHOTOGRAPHER | Just Loomis

COPYWRITER | Alan Schulman

CLIENT | Hart Marx Corporation

PAPER/PRINTER | Teton, Quintessence

This buyer's guide juxtaposes famous American authors,
businessmen, and visionaries with its fall line. It asks,
"How will you be remembered?"

DESIGN FIRM | Mires Design, Inc.

ART DIRECTOR | Jose Serrano

DESIGNER | Jose Serrano

CLIENT | Ethel M

The brochure was printed using a 4-color offset process.

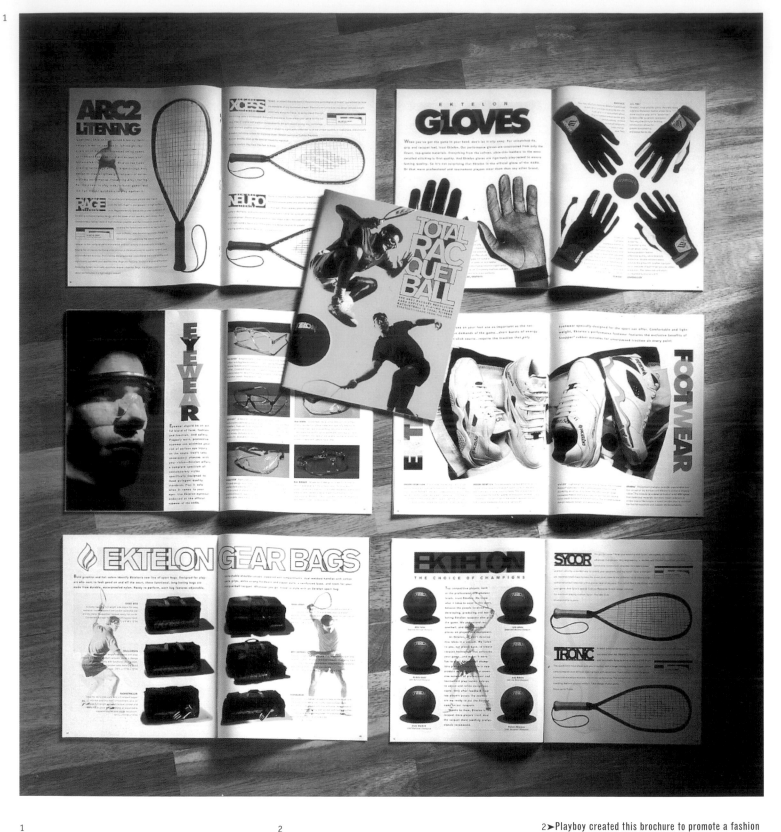

1

DESIGN FIRM | Mires Design

ART DIRECTOR | Jose Serrano

DESIGNER | Jose Serrano and Mike Brower

PHOTOGRAPHER | Carl Vanderschult

CLIENT | Ektelon

2

DESIGN FIRM | Playboy

ART DIRECTOR | Marise Mizrahi

DESIGNER | Marise Mizrahi

COPYWRITER | Irv Kornblau

CLIENT | Playboy Magazine

PAPER | Cover 100 lb. cover

TOOLS | Adobe Illustrator

2➤Playboy created this brochure to promote a fashion event in New York. The cover uses five colors and a dull and gloss varnish to achieve its effect. The firm distributed the brochures with 2-color invitations that open to a 1-color map of the New York subway printed on vellum.

The Playboy Fashion Interview

Andrew Fezza

Alexand...

Stuart Glasser

Bill Robinson

Nino Cerruti

Joseph Abbou...

Ronaldus Shamask

Ken Hoffman

1

1

DESIGN FIRM | Caldera Design
ART DIRECTOR | Paul Caldera
DESIGNER | Tim Fisher
PHOTOGRAPHER | Bob Carey
COPYWRITER | Imagineering
CLIENT | Teva, Deckers
TOOL | QuarkXPress

2

DESIGN FIRM | Hornall Anderson Design Works, Inc.
ART DIRECTOR | John Hornall
DESIGNERS | John Hornall, Mary Chin Hutchison,
  and Viola Lehr
ILLUSTRATOR | Gargoyles stock file
PHOTOGRAPHERS | Darrell Peterson and Stewart Tilger
COPYWRITER | Bill Bailey Carter
CLIENT | Gargoyles Performance Eyewear
PAPER | Vintage Gloss
TOOLS | QuarkXPress and Adobe Photoshop

2

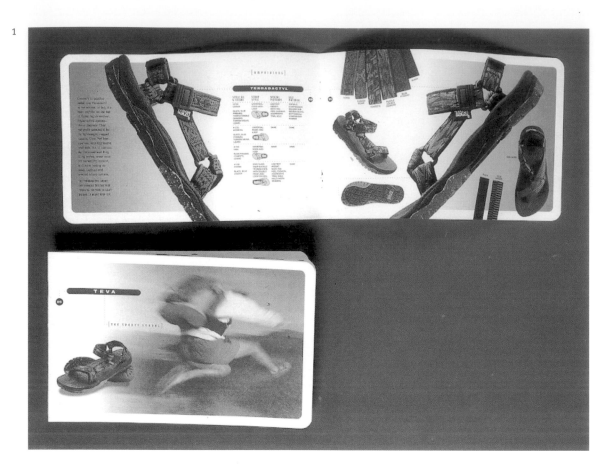

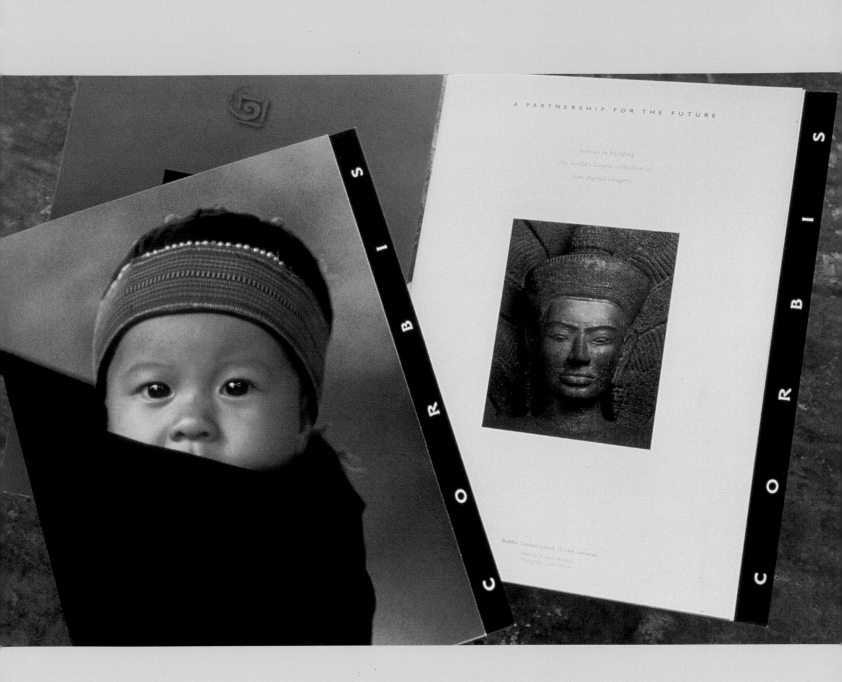

DESIGN FIRM | Hornall Anderson Design Works, Inc.

ART DIRECTOR | Jack Anderson

DESIGNER | Jack Anderson, John Anicker, and David Bates

PHOTOGRAPHY | Corbis stock archives

COPYWRITER | Lisa Marie Ford

CLIENT | Corbis

PAPER/PRINTER | Vintage Velvet

TOOLS | QuarkXPress, Adobe Photoshop,
   and Macromedia FreeHand

DESIGN FIRM | Sagmeister, Inc.

ART DIRECTOR | Stefan Sagmeister

DESIGNERS | Stefan Sagmeister and Eric Zim

ILLUSTRATOR | Eric Zim

PHOTOGRAPHER | Tom Schierlitz

COPYWRITER | Stephan Schertler

CLIENT | Schertler Audio Transducers

PAPER/PRINTER | 80 lb. Matte Coated, Cover Chipboard

Robert Kushner Schertler manufactures high-end audio pick-ups for acoustic instruments. Their logo is made up of concentric ellipses. Each chapter shows a photographic presentation of the logo.

DESIGN FIRM | Sibley/Peteet
ART DIRECTOR | Don Sibley
DESIGNER | Don Sibley
COPYWRITER | Kevin Johnson
CLIENT | Weyerhaeuser
PAPER/PRINTER | Weyerhaeuser Jaguar, Woods Lithographics

DESIGN FIRM | Sagmeister, Inc.
ART DIRECTORS | Stefan Sagmeister
  and Gunther Hrazdijra
DESIGNER | Stefan Sagmeister
PHOTOGRAPHER | Elfie Semothan
COPYWRITER | Gunther Hrazdijra
CLIENT | Motiva Studio
PAPER/PRINTER | Vogue, Germany

This brochure for a fashion show at the Museum of Modern Art in Vienna draws you to the show because the brochure itself was shot in the museum.

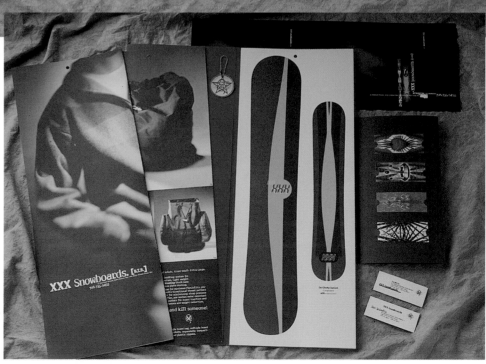

DESIGN FIRM | Segura, Inc.

ART DIRECTOR | Carlos Segura

DESIGNER | Carlos Segura

ILLUSTRATORS | Tony Klassen and Carlos Segura

PHOTOGRAPHER | Jeff Sciortino

CLIENT | Snowboards

PAPER/PRINTER | Bradley

TOOLS | Adobe Illustrator, QuarkXPress,
Adobe Photoshop, Ray Dream Designer

DESIGN FIRM | Hornall Anderson
Design Works, Inc.

ART DIRECTOR | Jack Anderson

DESIGNERS | Jack Anderson,
Bruce Branson-Meyer, Larry Anderston

COPYWRITER | Pamela Mason-Davey

CLIENT | Novell, Inc.

PAPER/PRINTING | Warren Lustro dull/
Grossberg Tyler

This corporate identity brochure was designed to serve as
an internal piece containing rationale for use and treatment
of the Novell identity. The standards bring a warm and
friendly meaning to the Novell identity. Photo images were
used to illustrate the connecting of people-to-people,
emphasizing the human element of technology.

Mathematica art images generated by simple programs based on two-dimensional colored noise (all by I. Bakshee).

DESIGN FIRM | Wolfram Research Creative Services

ART DIRECTOR | John Bonadies

DESIGNERS | John Bonadies, Jody Jasinski

ILLUSTRATOR | Michael Trott

COPYWRITER | Stephen Wolfram

CLIENT | Wolfram Research, Inc.

TOOLS | Mathematica, Adobe Illustrator, Adobe Photoshop, QuarkXPress

PAPER | Warren 70 lb. dull

This brochure's purpose is to communicate, in a manner that is comprehensive as well as easily understood, the features and extensive functionality of Mathematica 3.0, a fully integrated technical computing software package.

WOLFRAM RESEARCH

A First Look At MATHEMATICA® 3.0

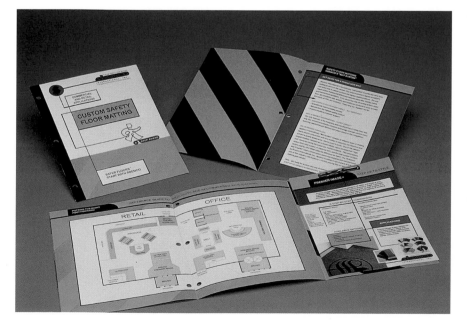

DESIGN FIRM | Sayles Graphic Design

ALL DESIGN | John Sayles

COPYWRITER | Wendy Lyons

CLIENT | Sbemco International

PAPER/PRINTING | Springhill/Offset printing

As part of an ongoing identity campaign, the piece features the Step Ahead theme. The piece includes the use of the company's trademarked fuchsia and teal backing. Designed to be flexible, the catalog has a metal fastener which attaches individual pages with details on specific product lines.

DESIGN FIRM | Greteman Group

ART DIRECTORS/DESIGNERS | Sonia Greteman, James Strange

COPYWRITER | Nita Scrivner

CLIENT | Learjet

TOOLS | Macromedia FreeHand

PAPER/PRINTING | Reflections/Offset printing

This workhorse, four-panel product brochure lends itself well to Learjet's family of aircrafts. Readers open to Lear-jet's overall story, then move on to pages that highlight each of the three jets. Strong bars of color separate the planes and help readers access the information they need. Two varnishes add richness to the photography and illustrations.

DESIGN FIRM | Brevis/KD Computer Graphics

ART DIRECTOR | Ralf Baumer

DESIGNER | Klaus-Dieter Nagel

CLIENT | Siemens Nixdorf

TOOLS | CorelDraw, Adobe Photoshop

PRINTING | Offset

The brochure describes the Middleware solution from Siemens Nixdorf, the largest European IT manufacturer. It was totally designed by using CorelDraw and Photoshop.

DESIGN FIRM | Giorgio Rocco Communications

ART DIRECTOR/DESIGNER | Giorgio Rocco

CLIENT | Giorgio Armani Parfums

TOOLS | Macintosh, Adobe PageMaker,
Macromedia FreeHand

PAPER/PRINTING | Colors/Fedigoni 300 gm paper/
Four-color process plus one PMS

This brochure was printed using four-color process with embossed simulation to give emphasis to the brand logotype. The pages have been tied with circular dark-gray metal buttons that key the special fifth color used within the brochure.

SOM MONETS HAVE

-en klassiker, der bevarer sin værdi over tiden

Pondocillin® pivampicillin

DESIGN FIRM | Department 058

ART DIRECTOR/DESIGNER | Vibeke Nodskov

CLIENT | Leo Pharmaceuticals

PAPER | Royal Consort 200 gm silk

The brochure required great attention from the printers, both in respect to the die cut and gluing as well as the spot varnish on both the cover and the interior.

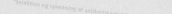

NORMALFLORAEN ER VÆRD AT KÆMPE FOR...

"Selektion og spredning af antibiotikaresistente bakterier.

Selektion og spredning af resistente bakterier sker først og fremmest ved antibiotikapåvirkning af den normale bakterieflora på hud og slimhinder. Alle antibiotika påvirker normalfloraen, om end i varierende grad. Smalspektrede antibiotika som penicillin V og dicloxacillin har begrænsede skadevirkninger på normalfloraen og selekterer kun i ringe grad for antibiotikaresistens. Bredspektrede antibiotika som tetracykliner, quinolones, cefalosporiner og sulfonamid kombineret med trimethoprim selekterer derimod hyppigt for antibiotikaresistens, herunder også multiresistens." [6,7]

Normalfloraens funktion er at beskytte mod fremmede mikroorganismer [1]

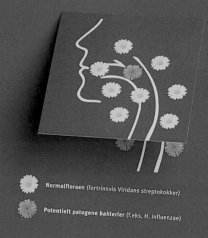

Normalfloraen (fortrinsvis Viridans streptokokker)

Potentielt patogene bakterier (f.eks. H. influenzae)

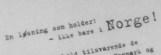

▲

DESIGN FIRM | Department 058

ART DIRECTOR/DESIGNER | Vibeke Nodskov

COPYWRITERS | Vibeke Nodskov,
Willy A. Nielsen

CLIENT | Leo Norway

PAPER | Royal Consort Silk

A unique twist on the usual four-color
process was the substitution of the
process yellow with PMS 803, so that
the look would be fluorescent.

◄

DESIGN FIRM | Toni Schowalter Design

ART DIRECTOR/DESIGNER | Toni Schowalter

CLIENT | Johnson and Johnson

TOOLS | Macintosh, QuarkXPress,
Adobe Illustrator, Adobe Photoshop

A square format, graphic cropping of
images with metallic inks, and duotones
create interest in this barrel-folded
brochure for Johnson and Johnson. The
piece compares the value of this division
with the consumer-products division.

ECC International

NEW GENERATION
FINE HIGH BRIGHTNESS
COATING CLAYS
FROM ECC INTERNATIONAL

DESIGN FIRM | Bluestone Design
DESIGNER | Ian Gunningham
ILLUSTRATOR | Symon Sweet
CLIENT | ECC International
TOOLS | Macintosh
PRINTING | Lithography

The client's product is
a new, super high-brightness
clay-coated paper. The design
needed to communicate gloss,
speed on print run, quality,
and high performance. Hence,
the use of winter time images.

paper gloss

print

gloss

Advanced pigment engineering
techniques have been used to
produce fine particle size
products which increase
paper gloss and maintain the
high deltagloss, or "snap",
characteristic of English
clays which is particularly
appropriate for the production
of high quality silk and
matt papers.

Paper Gloss /
Litho Ink Gloss

60 gsm LWC
offset coat
weight 10 gsm
Latex/CMC
formulation

The new generation English
clays give excellent coating
holdout and retain very good
coverage properties which
contribute to excellent offset
print performance. This is
both in terms of dry/litho print
density and a well-controlled
ink setting rate.

Ink Setting Rate (10s)

60 gsm LWC
offset coat
weight 10 gsm
Latex/CMC
formulation

Litho Print Density

60 gsm LWC
offset coat
weight 10 gsm
Latex/CMC
formulation

▶

DESIGN FIRM | Mason Charles Design

ART DIRECTOR/DESIGNER | Jeffrey Speiser

ILLUSTRATORS | Design Works,
Jeffrey Speiser

COPYWRITER | Kim Kovel

CLIENT | Belowzero

TOOLS | QuarkXPress, Adobe
Illustrator, Adobe Photoshop

PAPER/PRINTING | Valorem 65 lb.
opaque vellum/Job Parilux

Each year, the client prints a brochure
highlighting its winter clothing line. This
year a design was proposed that would involve
creating a plus-fold brochure. In order to include
pricing, descriptions, and trade show schedules,
a square was inserted that could be customized,
depending on the recipient.

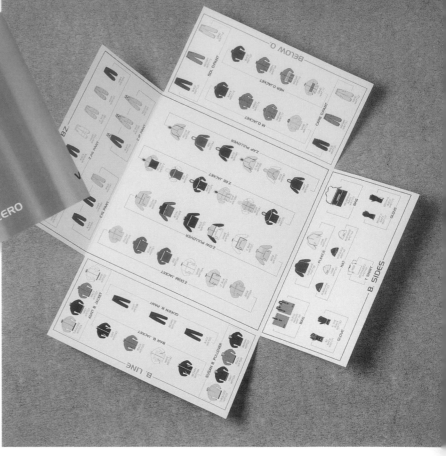

◀

DESIGN FIRM | Marketing and
Communications Strategies, Inc.

ART DIRECTOR | Lloyd Keels

DESIGNER | Eric Dean Freese

ILLUSTRATORS | Eric Dean Freese, Lloyd Keels

COPYWRITER | Simone Grace

CLIENT | Ecolotree

TOOLS | Power Macintoish 8100,
Adobe Photoshop, Adobe Illustrator, QuarkX-
Press

PAPER/PRINTING | Cougar 100 lb. smooth/
Four-color offset

The client, Ecolotree, needed a brochure to
promote its product, Buffer in a Bag, a system to mail-order trees. The client needed
the brochure to include full-color photos
of its products' applications plus an order
form. From start-to-finish, including scans
and creating the Buffer-in-a-Bag logo, the
entire brochure was designed in one 14-
hour day. Knowing that the time constraint
would be an obstacle, the hard-to-reach
client put most of the editorial responsibility on the MCS staff. The printing was
turned around in record time, and the
client was ecstatic about how quickly the
piece was completed.

DESIGN FIRM | Hornall Anderson Design Works, Inc.

ART DIRECTOR | Jack Anderson

DESIGNERS | Jack Anderson, Lisa Cerveny,
Suzanne Haddon

ILLUSTRATOR | Mits Katayama

COPYWRITER | Suky Hutton

CLIENT | Jamba Juice

PAPER/PRINTING | Simpson 65 lb. Sundance/Lithographix

The Jamba Juice Company is a leading retail purveyor of blended-to-order smoothies, fresh-squeezed juices, and health snacks. To communicate the client's objective, a palette of bright colors that appear throughout the stores and their collateral materials was used.

DESIGN FIRM | Pensare Design Group Ltd.

ART DIRECTOR | Mary Ellen Vehlow

DESIGNER | Camille Song

ILLUSTRATOR | Tim Flynn

CLIENT | World Bank

TOOLS | QuarkXPress, Adobe Photoshop,
Macromedia FreeHand, Adobe Illustrator

PAPER/PRINTING | Cover: Phoenix Imperial 110 lb./
Four-color process

The purpose of this brochure is to inform and promote global
bonds to the Japanese market. The challenge was to present the
visual information without offending any of the represented
countries and without any supplied art.

DESIGN FIRM | Sibley/Peteet Design

ART DIRECTOR/DESIGNER | Don Sibley

CLIENT | Weyerhaeuser Paper Company

This series of brochures for Weyerhaeuser Paper Company promotes their Cougar Offset grade and is part of an ongoing "American Artifacts" campaign. The piece is geared toward graphic designers and printers, and focuses on innovative printing techniques.

DESIGN FIRM | Palmquist and Palmquist

ART DIRECTORS/DESIGNERS | Kurt Palmquist, Denise Palmquist

ILLUSTRATORS | Selisa Rausch, Kurt Palmquist

COPYWRITER | Joann DeMeritt

CLIENT | Bridger Snowboard Gear

TOOLS | Adobe Illustrator

PAPER/PRINTING | Productolith Dull/Four-color process

The goal was to create a piece that would set Bridger Snowboard gear apart from the more funky snowboard wear companies. The designers focused on the functionality of the outerwear while still keeping in step with style.

DESIGN FIRM | Labbe Design

ART DIRECTORS | Jeff Labbe, Jon Gothold

DESIGNERS | Jeff Labbe, Marilyn Louthan

ILLUSTRATOR | CSA Archive

COPYWRITERS | Eric Springer, Ed Crayton

CLIENT | Qualcomm Inc.

TOOLS | Adobe Illustrator, QuarkXPress

PAPER/PRINTING | French Paper Co.

The challenge of the project was to make the reader aware of the problems of analog cellular phones and the vast improvement of digital cellular. By breaking down the communication through a number of pages, the reader has to struggle through an analog conversation. The brochure uses a secret/official theme that plays upon the fact that this technology was first used by spies in the 1940s. The pocket envelope contains a spec card that explains the new QCP-800.

DESIGN FIRM | Juice Design
ART DIRECTOR | Tery Young
DESIGNER | Brett M. Crithlow
COPYWRITER | Jon Schleuning
CLIENT | The Northface
Paper | Simpson Coronado 80
lb. White Stipple

This brochure was designed for the North Face's Freeport, Maine store. Its function was to advertise the store's location while offering local spots to test the gear out.

For thirty years, athletes whose lives depend on the performance of their gear have consistently chosen The North Face. We carry the expedition-proven tents, packs, sleeping bags, technical outerwear, skiwear and performance clothing that are the choice of the world's finest mountaineers, skiers and adventurers.

You'll find technical outdoor clothing and equipment, plus savings up to 60% on discontinued merchandise, seconds and overruns. All of our products are backed with The North Face Lifetime Warranty. You don't have to go far to get away.

Come to the store. Then please, go away.

While you're in Freeport, make The North Face your first stop before heading out to explore the area. Here are a few local areas for mountain biking, climbing and hiking adventures:

Camden Hills State Park: Camden, ME (45 miles north of Freeport) The park offers many miles of great trails to hike, some amazing views of the Atlantic, and a terrific climbing area known as Maiden's Cliff. For info call 207.287.

Grafton Notch Area: White Mountain Region near Bethel, Maine (2 hours) The Grafton Notch area features some of the most spectacular and rugged hiking in the Appalachians, including Mahoosuc Notch, rated the most difficult For more info call the Maine State Information Offi

Sunday River Mountain Bike Park: Bethel, Maine (2 hours northwest Sunday River's two chairlifts offer access to more than 60 miles miles of backroads and logging tracks to explore. For

rob hutchingson climbing in zion. photo: jim thornburg

high camp in the ak-su with alex lowe & conrad anker. photo: chris noble.

The North Face is located at 5 Bow Street and Main, Freeport, Maine.

Freeport, Maine

DESIGN FIRM | Widmeyer Design

ART DIRECTOR/DESIGNER | Dale Hart

ILLUSTRATOR | Christopher Downs

PHOTOGRAPHY | Landreth Studios

COPYWRITER | Seattle Software Labs

CLIENT | Seattle Software Labs

TOOLS | Power Macintosh,
Adobe Photoshop, Macromedia FreeHand

PAPER/PRINTING | Mead Signature Gloss/
Four-color process

Seattle Software Labs designs and manufactures Internet and computer-network security products. The gatefold brochure describes the increasing need for Internet and network security for businesses. Single page companion inserts outline specific product features and software options. The inserts were designed to accommodate both 8-1/2" x 11" and A4 formats for domestic and international use.

DESIGN FIRM | Studio MD

ART DIRECTOR/DESIGNER | Randy Lim

CLIENT | Chateau Ste. Michelle
Vineyards and Winery

TOOLS | Macromedia FreeHand,
Adobe Photoshop

PAPER/PRINTING | Warren Lustro
dull Recycled/Offset printing

This brochure announced the premier of the Chateau Ste. Michelle "Artist Series" wine collection featuring internationally acclaimed artist, Dale Chihuly. Each wine bottle in the six-bottle collection has a distinct label that depicts an exquisite Chihuly glass form. For the brochure, an accordion fold format was selected in order to showcase each of artist's glass sculptures on full-bleed panels.

DESIGN FIRM | Tom Fowler, Inc.

ART DIRECTORS | Thomas G. Fowler, Karl S. Maruyama

DESIGNERS | Thomas G. Fowler, Karl S. Maruyama,
Brien O'Reilly

COPYWRITER | Karl S. Maruyama

CLIENT | Canson-Talens, Inc.

TOOLS | QuarkXPress, Adobe Illustrator

PAPER | Utopia Premium Blue White 110 lb. cover,
Canson Satin (various weights)

PRINTING PROCESS | Offset, stamping, embossing,
and die-cutting

The goal of this brochure is to make the user aware
of all the unique possibilities of translucent paper, and
among translucent sheets, the superiority of Canson Satin.

DESIGN FIRM | Kan & Lau Design Consultants
ART DIRECTOR | Kan Tai-Keung
DESIGNERS | Kan Tai-Keung, Yu Chi Kong, Leung Dai Yin
CHINESE INK ILLUSTRATOR | Kan Tai-Keung
PHOTOGRAPHER | C. K. Wong
CHINESE ILLUSTRATORS | Kwun Tin Yau, Leung Wai Yin,
Tam Mo Fa
CLIENT | Tokushu Paper Manufacturing Co. Ltd.
TOOLS | Macromedia FreeHand, Adobe Photoshop,
Live Picture
PAPER | Bornfree recycled paper

The idea of using Bornfree recycled paper derived from a philosophy of Buddhism: economize to protect the Chinese market. Inspired from this philosophy, elements of calligraphy were applied to demonstrate the printing aspects of the paper series.

"BORNFREE" CONNOTES A FREE AND EASY LIFE-

STYLE THAT IS HARMONIOUS WITH NATURE,

BACKED BY A PHILOSOPHICAL LINKAGE WITH
《自在》乃中國佛家思想中的一種生活哲理：
CHINESE BUDDHISM THINKING. CATERING TO
逍遙自在，無憂無礙，與大自然和諧共處。
THE CHINA MARKET, THE DESIGN OF "BORNFREE"
《自在》花紋紙系列是特別為中國市場面
PAPER SERIES IS DERIVED FROM THE IDEA OF
設計的紙張。意念來自中國傳統手造紙的毛
BAMBOO GRAINED SURFACE AND TEAR-OFF EDGES
邊和竹紋肌理，以自然的變化構成自由的韻
OF TRADITIONAL CHINESE HAND-MADE PAPER.
律，表現中國人悠然自得的生活精神。
THE TEXTURE ENHANCES A NATURAL, BRISK

AND RHYTHMICAL APPEAL WHICH REPRESENTS

A PART OF THE CHINESE CAREFREE LIFESTYLE.

herbasis™

DESIGN FIRM | Design Guys

ART DIRECTOR | Steven Sikora

DESIGNERS | Jay Theige, Amy Kirkpatrick

PHOTOGRAPHERS | Darrell Eager, Michael Crouser

COPYWRITERS | Jay Kaskel, Steven Sikora

CLIENT | Target Stores

PRINTING PROCESS | Offset lithography

Due to the client's limited advertising budget, a great deal of pressure was placed on this product brochure to completely define the brand character of Herbasis to consumers. The creative team kept the design simple and clean, but also used appropriate people and botanicals to add dimension and mystique.

well beyond beauty™

RENEGADE
LIGHTING & FURNITURE

RENEGADE
HARDWARE

DESIGN FIRM | Creative Conspiracy Inc.

ART DIRECTOR | Chris Hickcox

DESIGNER | Neil Hannum

PHOTOGRAPHER | Laurie Dickson

CLIENT | Renegade Artful Objects

TOOLS | QuarkXPress, Adobe Photoshop

PRINTING PROCESS | Four-color process

The design team showcased each item individually to allow the viewer to focus on details. Influences for the design came from colors and textures found in nature.

DESIGN FIRM | Shields Design
ART DIRECTORS | Stephanie Wong, Charles Shields
DESIGNER | Charles Shields
PHOTOGRAPHER | Keith Seaman-Camerad
CLIENT | Innerspace Industries
TOOLS | Adobe Illustrator and Photoshop
PRINTING PROCESS | Four-color

The client wanted a series of brochures highlighting different furniture lines. The designers came up with a color-coding system to identify each line. Color-coding also saved money by allowing two-over-four printing.

DESIGN FIRM | Visual Marketing Associates, Inc.
ART DIRECTORS | Tracy Meiners, Ken Botts
DESIGNER | Tracy Meiners
ILLUSTRATOR | Cliff Parsons
PHOTOGRAPHER | Jim France, France Photography; stock
COPYWRITER | Pamela Cordery
CLIENT | Suncast Corporation
TOOLS | Macromedia FreeHand, Adobe Photoshop
PAPER | Mead Sig-Nature 80 lb. cover
PRINTING PROCESS | Six-color plus off-line varnish,
dry-trapped, offset lithography

The embossed cover reflects the unique mold pattern of the Just Stuff product line. Large lifestyle imagery adds a playful human element, and is Quadtoned, allowing focus on the product. Kraft paper hints at the product packaging, while providing a neutral backdrop for specific information.

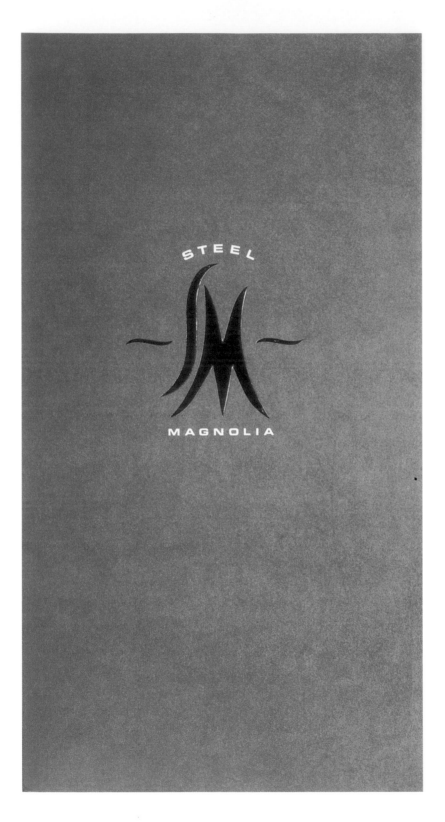

DESIGN FIRM | Big Eye Creative, Inc.
ART DIRECTOR/DESIGNER | Asiza Ilicic
PHOTOGRAPHER | Dann Ilicic
COPYWRITER | Craig Holm
CLIENT | Steel Magnolia
TOOLS | QuarkXPress, Adobe Photoshop
PAPER | Centura Gloss
PRINTING PROCESS | Four-color with spot tint varnish

This catalogue was designed to convey the delicate elegance of Steel Magnolia's custom metal furniture, while balancing the icy strength of the steel they use in all of their creations. Since interior designers are their biggest customers, the catalogue had to be refined, exclusive, and of the finest quality.

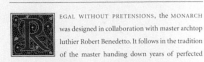

The Monarch

EGAL WITHOUT PRETENSIONS, the MONARCH was designed in collaboration with master archtop luthier Robert Benedetto. It follows in the tradition of the master handing down years of perfected methods and designs to his apprentice. ■ Possessing all the features of the ARTISAN, the MONARCH boasts several attractive additions. Crowning this guitar is a large Benedetto-style headstock with mitred purflings and pinstripe-enhanced binding. The f-holes are fully bound and also trimmed with mitred pinstriped purflings. Only the finest quartersawn seasoned instrument woods are used in its construction, and as with every archtop guitar in the Buscarino lineage the MONARCH is meticulously assembled and tuned. ■ A long list of options and color choices (including the sunburst finish shown opposite), allow the MONARCH to be custom designed as a guitar fit for a king.

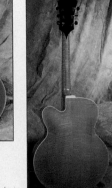

Honey Blonde MONARCH

MONARCH back, showing triple-A wood in a Honey Blonde finish.

6

THE MONARCH

DESIGN FIRM | Ken Weightman Design
ART DIRECTOR/DESIGNER | Ken Weightman
CLIENT | Buscarino Guitars
TOOLS | QuarkXPress, Adobe Photoshop
PRINTING PROCESS | Offset, die-cut, liquid laminate cover

Liquid laminate on the cover's full-size image suggests the finish of the actual guitars. The F-hole is die-cut. Inside, each of the handcrafted guitar models is presented as fine art.

Drawing from Life

DESIGN FIRM | Pensare Design Group, Ltd.
ART DIRECTOR | Mary Ellen Vehlow
DESIGNERS | Camille Song, Amy Billingham
COPYWRITERS/CLIENT | Devin O'Brien, Adam Attenderfer
TOOLS | Adobe Illustrator and Photoshop, QuarkXPress
PAPER | Monadnock Dulcet, Bier Papier Ale
PRINTING PROCESS | Four-color; silver, white, black on cover

The purpose of this catalog is to showcase the works of the untrained artists of Kenya. The concept was to make readers feel as if they had journeyed into the lives of these children and this is a scrapbook of their adventures.

David Kinywa

David is 19 years old and has been a part of Streetwise since its beginning in January 1994. He was one of the first to get a job painting for a carpentry business. He began working there part-time in April 1995, but they recently refused to make him a permanent employee. He has now returned to Streetwise where he is one of the top designers.

The nomadic Maasai are people of the land. Their survival depends upon the herding of cattle and the harvesting of its milk and blood.

DESIGN FIRM | Hornall Anderson Design Works, Inc.

ART DIRECTORS | Jack Anderson, Lisa Cerveny

DESIGNERS | Jack Anderson, Lisa Cerveny, Mary Hermes, Jana Nishi, Virginia Le, Jana Wilson Esser

ILLUSTRATOR | Dave Julian

PHOTOGRAPHER | Tom Collicott

COPYWRITER | Suky Hutton

CLIENT | Mohawk Paper Mills

TOOLS | Macromedia FreeHand, Adobe Illustrator, QuarkXPress

PAPER | Mohawk Tomahawk

The booklet features the best characteristics of the Tomahawk line by appealing to the reader's senses of smell, sight, touch, hearing, and taste. Humor was used to showcase the client's versatile Tomahawk textured line, including optical illusions, insightful trivia, and scratch-and-sniff pages.

a new

take on an

old tradition

DESIGN FIRM | Muller and Co.

ALL DESIGN | Jeff Miller

COPYWRITERS | Lyric Opera

CLIENT | Lyric Opera

TOOLS | QuarkXPress, Macintosh

PRINTING PROCESS | Four-color offset

The imagery came from taking traditional elements, such as a rose, floral wallpaper, and patterns, then cutting, scratching, reversing, and replacing their original colors with bright, saturated hues.

DESIGN FIRM | **DIA**

ART DIRECTOR/DESIGNER | Andrew Cook

PHOTOGRAPHER | Vic Paris

COPYWRITER | Robert Davis

CLIENT | AD&D

PAPER | Mohawk

PRINTING PROCESS | Lithography

The catalogue clearly demonstrates the range of products through photographic and graphic styles.

Mark Morris Dance Group

The Classics

TIMELESS WORKS OF ART

CHANTICLEER

These 12 men comprise an orchestra of voices. The sheer beauty of their sound stems from a seamless blend of carefully matched male voices, ranging from resonant bass to purest countertenor. The ensemble has thrilled audiences worldwide with its brilliance and its repertoire, which includes everything from Renaissance to jazz, gospel to new music. The only full-time classical voice ensemble in this country, Chanticleer has developed a remarkable reputation over an 18-year history for its interpretation of vocal literature. Revel as they do in the pleasure of song.
Sunday, October 6, 7:30pm
$25, $22, $18

MARK MORRIS
DANCE GROUP

Here is one of the great choreographers of our time, considered a genius by many. His dance

reverberates with wit, humor and lucid musicality. He breaks all the rules, even his own. Irreverent, iconoclastic and yet his work reveals a seriousness and deep understanding of dance. Morris is intensely musical, miraculously turning the classical works of Haydn and Vivaldi into the most contemporary of dances. According to *The Los Angeles Times*, Mark Morris "is deceptively cerebral, insinuatingly sensual, fabulously funky," Now, in the prime of his career, you can see the miracle of Mark Morris.
Sunday–Monday, October 13–14, 7:30pm
$35, $32, $27.50

MOSCOW FESTIVAL
BALLET

Combining the best classical elements of two extraordinary companies, the Bolshoi and the Kirov, Artistic Director Sergei Radchenko has forged an exciting new company with some of Russia's leading dancers, including Prima

13

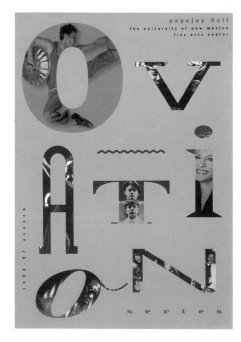

DESIGN FIRM | Vaughn Wedeen Creative
ART DIRECTOR/DESIGNER | Rick Vaughn
PHOTOGRAPHER | UNM Public Events Management
COPYWRITER | UNM Public Events Management
CLIENT | UNM Public Events Management
PAPER | Cougar Opaque White 80 lb. text
PRINTING PROCESS | Four-color process

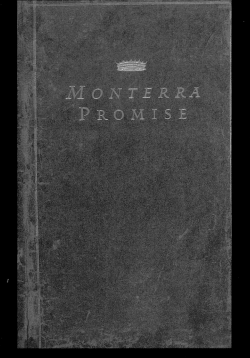

DESIGN FIRM | Louisa Sugar Design
ART DIRECTOR | Louisa Sugar
DESIGNERS | Louisa Sugar, Melissa Nery
ILLUSTRATORS | Joey Mantre, Greg Spalenka
COPYWRITER | Lee Nordlund
CLIENT | Monterra Promise Proprietor-Grown Wines
TOOLS | QuarkXPress
PAPER | Teton, Starwhite Vicksburg
PRINTING PROCESS | Letterpress, hot stamping, offset
lithography

Research into the place where Monterra Promise wine grapes are grown uncovered a fascinating history, beginning with discovery of the land by the King of Spain' explorers in the 1600s. To communicate these historical roots, this launch brochure was designed to look like a rare book from that era.

MONTERRA
PROMISE

GRAPES FROM
THE
BEST VINTAGES ONLY
ARE SELECTED FOR
MONTERRA
PROPRIETOR GROWN WINES.

TOM SMITH   BILL PETROVIC
WINEMAKER   VINEYARD MANAGER

COLOGNE

Wear your own signature statement with these revitalizing colognes. Uniquely formulated with aloe vera, jojoba oil and essential oils, they refresh the skin while adding a layer of fragrance to complement your lifestyle.

75 ML / 2.5 FL OZ

02521 EUCALYPTUS
02522 LAVENDER
02523 VETIVER

GLYCERINE SOAP

Pure vegetable glycerine and fragrant essential extracts are the beginning of these beautifully scented jeweltone bars. Enriched with jojoba oil, honey and Vitamins A and E, the gentle lather cleanses thoroughly and then rinses away clean. Perfect for all skin types.

2 SOAPS – 85 G / 3 OZ EACH

02091 EUCALYPTUS
02092 LAVENDER
02093 VETIVER

FOAMING BATH

Surround yourself with pure herbal fragrances while mounds of bubbles delight your senses. Enriched with jojoba oil, aloe vera and Vitamin E, the copious foam creates a private sanctuary that leaves your skin feeling soft and renewed.

235 ML / 8 FL OZ

02071 EUCALYPTUS
02072 LAVENDER
02073 VETIVER

1-800-366-4071

DESIGN FIRM | Design Guys

ART DIRECTORS | Steven Sikora, Lynette Sikora, Gary Patch

DESIGNERS | Jay Theige, Amy Kirkpatrick

PHOTOGRAPHER | Patrick Fox

COPYWRITER | Jana Branch

CLIENT | The Thymes Limited

PRINTING PROCESS | Offset lithography

The inspiration for this catalog was the product packaging. Design Guys styled the brochure similar to the style of each collection, like a travel journal of different places. This entire book was shot in-studio, in natural daylight.

DESIGN FIRM | Factor Design
ART DIRECTOR/ILLUSTRATOR | Paul Neulinger
DESIGNER | Kristina Düllmann
PHOTOGRAPHER | Photodisc
COPYWRITER | Hannah S. Fricke
CLIENT | Römerturn Feinstpapier
TOOLS | Macromedia FreeHand, QuarkXPress, Macintosh
PAPER | Römerturm Kombination
PRINTING PROCESS | Four-color offset

This brochure introduces the new paper line of Römerturm Feinstpapier called Kombination. The big benefit of this new assortment is that it combines different surfaces and shades of white in one line of stock.

SÜDKURVE

In der Südkurve war mächtig was los. In den ersten sieben Spielminuten war noch kein Tor gefallen. Atemlos und ohne hinzusehen, drehte Fricke ihre Thermoskanne auf, und durch eine Wolke entschieden frischen Pfefferminzduftes konnte sie die Abseitsfalle gerade noch erkennen, die dem Schiedsrichter entgehen würde. Mist. Am spannendsten allerdings schien es auf den Rängen selbst zu werden. Das Stadion war so voll wie schon lange nicht mehr. Schräg gegenüber war ein ziemlicher Tumult zu erkennen, und die Ehrentribüne war ausnahmsweise einmal mehr als voll. »'TSCHULDIGUNG«. Zwischen Fricke und die Pfefferminzschwaden drängte sich eine Eintrittskarte. »DAS IST MEIN PLATZ.« Die Eintrittskarte verschwand, und statt ihrer tauchte das Gesicht eines Unsympathen auf, dem Fricke nicht einmal dann ihren Platz eingeräumt hätte, wenn sie nicht eine 1a-Dauerkarte gehabt hätte. »IRRTUM, MÄNNEKEN«, sagte eine hochaufgeschossene Kapuzenjacke. »DAS IST MEIN PLATZ. WENN ICH DANN MAL BITTEN DÜRFTE.« Fricke blieb wie ein Fels sitzen, als die Durchsage kam: »LIEBE FANS, OFFENBAR HAT EIN FÄLSCHERRING EINTRITTSKARTEN NACHDRUCKEN LASSEN. WIR BRECHEN DAS SPIEL DAHER AB. BITTE FOLGEN SIE DEN ANWEISUNGEN DER ORDNUNGSKRÄFTE. DANKE.« Das Stadion kochte. Die Fans hoben wütend ihre Wimpel und Schals – ein einziges Meer in Gelb und Grün.

DESIGN FIRM | SJI Associates

DESIGNER | Anthony Cinturatti

PHOTOGRAPHER | Client-supplied photos

COPYWRITERS | Kevin Rayman, Sarah Starr

CLIENT | General Cigar/Villazon

TOOLS | QuarkXPress, Adobe Illustrator and Photoshop

PAPER | Productolith

PRINTING PROCESS | Four-color offset, die-cut and die-scored

The client wanted a brochure that showed all the cigars in the Excalibur line in an exciting, non-traditional format. The use of alternating cream and black panels, duotones, and a short-fold cover create a warm, sophisticated look that appeals to the younger, fashionable cigar smoker.

PRIGMORE · KRIEVINS | *Architects*

DESIGN FIRM | Greteman Group
ART DIRECTORS | Sonia Greteman, James Strange
DESIGNER | Craig Tomson, James Strange
PHOTOGRAPHER | Paul Bowen
COPYWRITER | Deanna Harms
CLIENT | Learjet
TOOLS | Macromedia FreeHand, Adobe Photoshop
PAPER | Reflections
PRINTING PROCESS | Four-color process, spot metallic,
gloss varnish

This highly successful, four-color product brochure
communicates the Learjet 31A's key selling points
through stunning photography, graphs, fold outs, subtle
screens, and generous white space.

Notes for the Season

1997

SERVICE
BROCHURES

DESIGN FIRM Lee Reedy Creative, Inc.
ART DIRECTOR Lee Reedy
DESIGNER/ILLUSTRATOR Heather Haworth
COPYWRITER Jamie Reedy
CLIENT Frederic Printing
TOOLS QuarkXPress
PRINTING PROCESS Six-color with metallic silver

A holiday music CD was given to clients with
this brochure for diary notations about
Christmas dinners, gifts, and other holiday
pleasures. Handpainted graphics added to
the friendly mood of the holidays.

where
the
pavement
stops
chris haines
baja
off-road
tours
begin

DESIGN FIRM | Mike Salisbury Communications, Inc.
ART DIRECTOR | Mike Salisbury
DESIGNER | Mary Evelyn McGough
CLIENT | Chris Haines' Baja Off-Road Tours
TOOLS | QuarkXPress, Adobe Illustrator
PAPER/PRINTING | Duotone 50 lb. text, newsprint aged; Duotone 80 lb. cover, packing gray; saddle stitched-long side/Four-color process

Primary production was done using Quark and Illustrator. A fluorescent color was added to the front and back to add visual impact to the piece.

DESIGN FIRM | Rose Srebro Design
ART DIRECTOR | Rose Srebro
DESIGNERS | Rose Srebro, Chris Clarendon
CLIENT | Massport
TOOLS | QuarkXPress, Macromedia FreeHand
PAPER/PRINTING | Crosspoint Genesis/Emco Printers

This guide for tourists visiting Massachusetts offers a listing of entertainment, museums, and art. The primary design consideration was that all information was effectively communicated while being easy to read.

The **ARTS** in Massachusetts

The Best of the Bay State:

A Guide to Cultural Entertainment in

DESIGN FIRM | Metalli Lindberg Advertising

CREATIVE DIRECTOR | Lioneus Borean, Stefano Dal Tin

DESIGNER | Owen M. Walters

CLIENT | Bobadilla Athletic Center

TOOLS | Adobe Illustrator, Adobe Photoshop

This accordion-fold promotional piece for an important fitness center uses several type treatments to catch the viewer's eye. The piece was mailed to clients to promote new courses and activities.

DESIGN FIRM | Wdesign, Inc.

ART DIRECTOR | Alan Wallner

DESIGNER | Lisa Hagman

COPYWRITER | Sharon Feiner

CLIENT | Dorholt Printing

TOOLS | 3M Materials

Dorholt Printing needed a brochure that would highlight their many capabilities that were unknown in this competitive market. Now they are competing with the high-end printers in the area and business is booming.

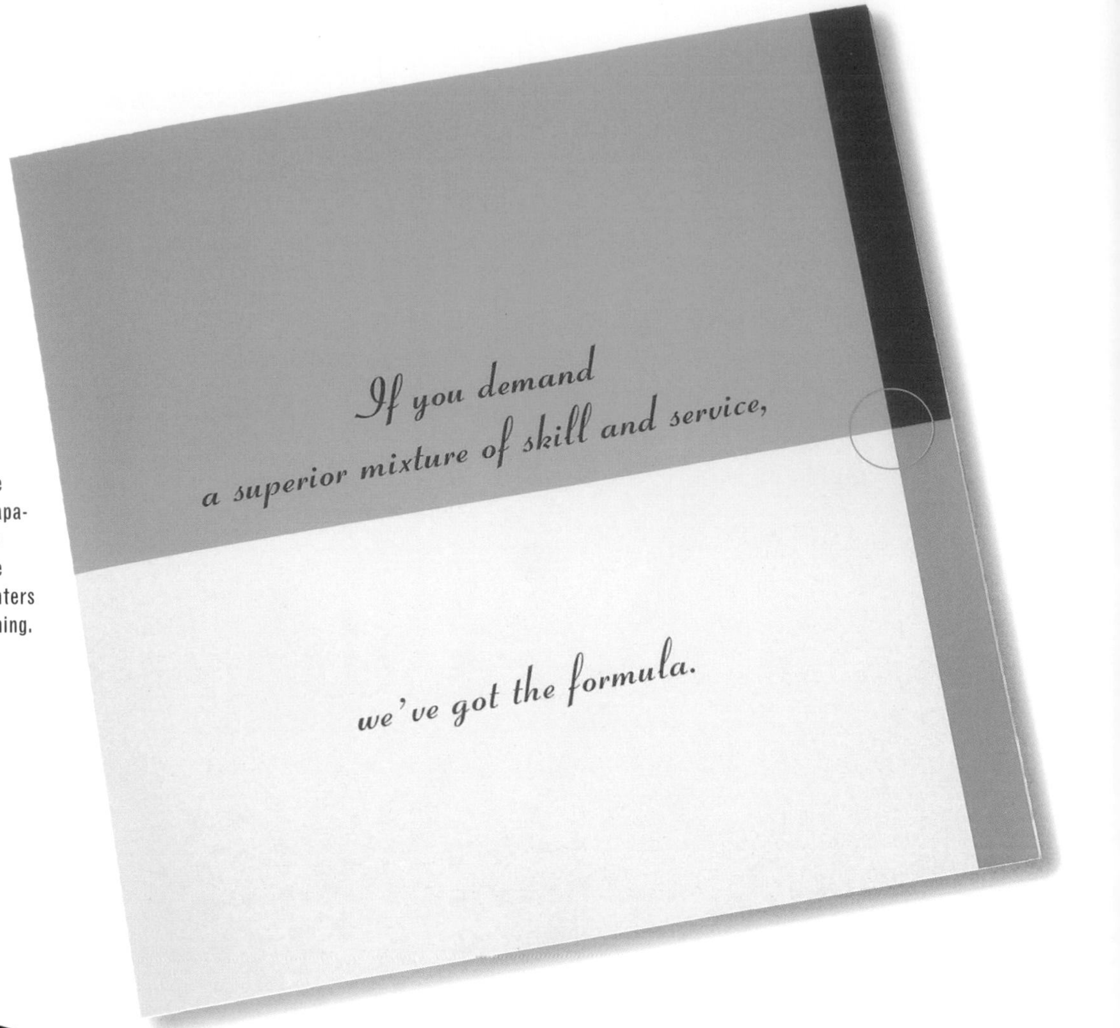

If you demand
a superior mixture of skill and service,

we've got the formula.

DESIGN FIRM | Design Center
ART DIRECTOR | John Reger
DESIGNER | Sherwin Schwartzrock
COPYWRITER | John Roberg
CLIENT | Spanlink
TOOLS | Macintosh, Macromedia FreeHand
PAPER/PRINTING | Warren Lustro, Olympic Printers

Using a light presentation with whimsical graphics, the piece's purpose is to show a problem with telephones and the solution. A special graphic is placed in die-cut form on the first page.

Still puzzling over the age-old call center problems?

Understaffing

DESIGN FIRM | TGD Communications

ART DIRECTOR | Rochelle Gray

ILLUSTRATOR | Judy Reed Silver

CLIENT | Food Marketing Institute

TOOLS | QuarkXPress

This promotional piece for a grocer's convention includes illustrations that were painted using acrylics and line work that was scanned into Photoshop and printed as an overlay on reflective art.

DESIGN FIRM | Clark Design

ART DIRECTOR | Annemarie Clark

DESIGNERS | Thurlow Wasam, Doug daSilva, Ozzie Paton, Carol Piechocki

COPYWRITER | Melanie Wellbeloved

CLIENT | KRON-TV

TOOLS | QuarkXPress, Adobe Photoshop, Adobe Illustrator

PRINTING | Indigo printing

The purpose of this sales piece was to inform media buyers that the client consisted of five independent sources for media placement. One challenge was to maintain each company's separate identity without isolating them from the parent company. This was accomplished by creating a single, spiral-bound brochure that contains a series of unique brochures, each representing one of the five independent companies. Indigo printing process was used to stay within the budget.

DESIGN FIRM | Tom Fowler, Inc.

ART DIRECTOR | Thomas G. Fowler

DESIGNER | Karl S. Maruyama

CLIENT | Herlin Press

TOOLS | QuarkXPress, Adobe Illustrator, Adobe Photoshop

PAPER/PRINTING | Fox River Confetti/ Herlin Press

The client needed a promotional piece to demonstrate advantages of direct-to-plate, short-run printing presses versus competing electronic imaging presses.

DESIGN FIRM | Sayles Graphic Design

ART DIRECTOR | John Sayles

DESIGNERS | John Sayles, Jennifer Elliott

ILLUSTRATOR | John Sayles

COPYWRITER | Annie Meacham

CLIENT | Timbuktuu Coffee Bar

PAPER/PRINTING | Chipboard and Curtis Tuscan Terra/ Screenprinting

For the grand opening of a new coffee bar with a rustic, native atmosphere, the invitation used "leftover" materials for texture and added special effects including a stir-stick and a small bag of coffee beans.

DESIGN FIRM | Oakley Design Studios
ART DIRECTOR/DESIGNER | Tim Oakley
ILLUSTRATORS | Mike Fraiser, Tim Oakley
COPYWRITER | Carri Bugbee
CLIENT | Mira Mobile Television
TOOLS | Macintosh
PAPER | Luna Gloss

DESIGN FIRM | Words of Art
ART DIRECTOR/DESIGNER | Sharon Feldstein
CLIENT | Camp Isidore Alterman of the
Atlanta Jewish Community Center
TOOLS | Adobe PageMaker, Adobe Illustrator
PAPER/PRINTING | NW 80 lb. gloss cover/four
spot colors

The client needed a summer-camp brochure
that would portray fun using color and
graphics, but not photos. Angled die cuts
and colors effectively separated categories for easy location of information.
A separate application was included and
mailed in a one-color printed envelope.

DESIGN FIRM | Hornall Anderson Design Works, Inc.

ART DIRECTOR | Jack Anderson

DESIGNERS | Jack Anderson, Lisa Cerveny, Jana Wilson, Julie Keenan

COPYWRITER | Jeff Fraga

CLIENT | XactData Corporation

PAPER/PRINTING | Strathmore Elements, Pin Stripe; Key Lithography

The primary objective for the XactData identity program was to create a sales piece that appeared technical, yet reader friendly. Initially, the client wanted to include illustrations, but a limited budget kept the program to two colors while illustrations were done in-house.

[XACTDATA]
LAN BACKUP
AND RECOVERY
Keep your data: Safely off-site. Conveniently on-line.
Automatically at XactData.

[The trouble with traditional network backup systems] Their data is inaccessible. **They depend on human intervention.** There is no simple, inexpensive way to get the data stored off-site for disaster recovery. **Tape systems are temperamental, mechanical devices.** Tape backup requires time-consuming and unreliable human intervention. **Data retrieval is difficult; immediate access next to impossible.** Hardware is continually made obsolete by advances in technology. **And the list goes on.**

[Introducing a new way to backup network data] A revolutionary way that keeps your data on-line at all times. **A secure way that stores your data safely off-site.** A reliable way that eliminates cumbersome tape backups. **A fail-safe way that has three levels of security.** An innovative way that uses high-speed digital communications. **A convenient way that's automatic and requires no human intervention.** We call it XactData, because it's exactly what you want in a network backup system.

BLUEPRINT FOR ACHIEVEMENT

THE STRATEGIC PLAN
OF THE INSURANCE INSTITUTE
FOR PROPERTY LOSS REDUCTION

SPONSORED BY THE INSURANCE INDUSTRY AND OTHERS COMMITTED TO ACCOMPLISHING OUR MISSION:
"REDUCING DEATHS, INJURIES, PROPERTY DAMAGE, ECONOMIC LOSSES, AND HUMAN SUFFERING CAUSED BY NATURAL DISASTERS."

DESIGN FIRM | KBB Communications Design

ART DIRECTOR | Jamie Bernard

DESIGNER/ILLUSTRATOR | Anna Bemis

COPYWRITER | Insurance Institute for Property
Loss Reduction

CLIENT | Institute for Property Loss Reduction

TOOLS | QuarkXPress, Adobe Illustrator

PAPER | Warren Lustro 80 lb.

Created to introduce the company's new strategic plan,
this piece fulfills the client's requirements of individual
icons to represent key strategic points.

#4 KEY RESULT AREA

RETROFIT EXISTING STRUCTURES

RETROFIT EXISTING STRUCTURES

Promote the strengthening of structures to mitigate natural disaster risks through a process called "retrofit".

Goals

▲ Cost-effective techniques for retrofitting existing structures will be developed by working with partners.

▲ Incentives will be established for all stakeholders to use these techniques to retrofit existing structures.

Example Strategies

1. Work with partners — governments, mortgage companies, and employers — to establish incentives which will encourage retrofit.

2. Promote retrofitting high "people" risk structures, public safety structures, life line structures and structures located in high-risk zones.

Key Initial Project

Work with partners to retrofit every public and non-profit child care center in the country.

KEY RESULT AREA #5

INFORMATION MANAGEMENT

Provide for the collection, analysis, and dissemination of natural disaster loss and mitigation information.

Goals

▲ A credible, accurate and comprehensive natural disaster risk, loss data, and mitigation information system will be developed.

▲ The information system will identify mitigation opportunities and future mitigation activities.

▲ Information products will be developed in a variety of formats for easy use by stakeholders.

2. Develop and maintain a database of insurer paid losses from natural disasters.

3. Develop and maintain a building code database to identify current practice, proposed actions, and potential actions for initiatives.

4. Develop and maintain an interactive World Wide Web site linked to other information sources.

Example Strategies

1. Maintain a comprehensive disaster loss data and mitigation information service that responds to member company request for information.

Key Initial Project

Provide a rapid and efficient means to distribute mitigation related data and cost-effective techniques to insurance company members and others.

INFORMATION MANAGEMENT

DESIGN FIRM | Barbara Brown Marketing and Design
ART DIRECTOR | Barbara Brown
DESIGNERS | Barbara Brown, Darthe Silver
COPYWRITER | Annie Hall
CLIENT | Jim Hall II Kart Racing Schools
PRINTING | Inland Litho

In the past, the client's promotional materials were very corporate in appearance. Using images related to the client's services, excitement of the sport was brought into the marketing materials through active colors and metal in the photos and type that produce the effect of motion.

JIM HALL II
KART RACING
SCHOOLS

WHEEL
to
WHEEL
RACING

Tight Turns
Fast
STRAIGHTAWAY
Speed

SPRINT
SHIFTER
RACING

805/654-1329

Easy reservations
805/654-1329

Real racers drive fast and smart. Drivers from the exclusive ranks of F-1, Indy Car and NASCAR emphasize kart racing's significance in their careers.

Skill, experience and meticulous training in race dynamics - - - kart racing paves the way for today's young talents world-wide. Local, statewide and national kart races showcase career drivers and weekend warriors.

Instructors at Jim Hall Kart Racing Schools skillfully apply their expertise immediately at your first session - the Introduction to Kart Racing program.

Advanced programs focus on braking points, inside/outside passing lines, developing quick

reaction skills, maintaining a consistent driving line. Preparing you for the decisive split second advantage, JHKRS divides podium finishers from all the rest. Multi-level race instruction is designed to unleash your racing talents, boosting your driving performance.

Karting is the most affordable motorsport today. More than 1,200 racing enthusiasts and skill-seekers per year graduate from Jim Hall Kart Racing Schools. JHKRS are fully sponsored with top of the line sprint and shifter karts and accessories.

Program tuition includes everything...all new race-ready karts, seat time, driver gear, insurance and expert one-on-one training. You benefit from

top professional instruction and lots of track time. Each course includes on-track racing with timed sessions, challenging drills, question and answer periods and a personal performance evaluation. Your only requirement is to be enthusiastic.

Jim Hall II formulates specific driving skills and drills for both the novice and expert racer. Winner of more than 200 kart races, his extensive motorsport credentials include national titles in kart racing to owning and running an Indy Car team. Jim Hall II has set a high standard among all racing schools in the United States.

Church METRO

catalog
of Media Resources

DESIGN FIRM | Design Center
ART DIRECTOR | John Reger
DESIGNER | John Erickson
COPYWRITER | Church Metro
CLIENT | Church Metro
TOOLS | Macintosh, Macromedia FreeHand
PAPER/PRINTING | Lustro/Printcraft

To entice the viewer to take a look inside, the designers used text (representing books) and earphones (for tapes). The goal was to take a serious subject and make it fun.

BUSINESS
LEADERSHIP

Books

Becoming a Woman of Excellence

Cynthia Heald

In this motivating Bible study, married and single women can discover what they should be striving for with God's excellence as a model. If you're hungry for God's perspective on success in a society that bombards you with conflicting demands, feed on the truths of God's Word that you'll discover in this book. You will not only learn to "approve the things that are excellent," but you will experience the joy of becoming God's woman of excellence.
Order Code: HEAHWEB
Price: $7.00

Life Launch: A Passionate Guide to the Rest of Your Life

Frederic M. Hudson & Pamela D. McLean

Are you better off today, at being who you are, than you were a year ago? At work? At home? There are not many blueprints of safety nets guiding our lives in our turbulent world of constant surprises. You have to create your own. In our turbulent world, our lives and careers must be redesigned over and over again as we live them. Few know how to do this, as they shift gears in the endless churning of complex change. Life Launch provides the tools you need to author your future, no matter what your age and situation. You will learn to facilitate optimal choices within your own vision and reach weaving together personal and professional plans around your deep sense of purpose.
Order Code: HUDLPB
Price: $16.95

The Case for Christianity

C.S. Lewis

This is Lewis at his best. He presents the case for Christian belief in two parts, "Right and Wrong as a Clue to the Meaning of the Universe" and "What Christians Believe." With all the power of his formidable intellect and his legendary wit, C.S. Lewis condenses the arguments for the reasonableness of Christian faith in an admirable, concise, and compelling presentation.
Order Code: LEWCFCB
Price: $5.95

The Seven Habits of Highly Effective People

Stephen R. Covey

This book has been a national bestseller for several years, with more than 30 million copies in print. Now available in 17 languages and 39 countries, this enlightening book teaches how to get more fulfillment from your time, your relationships—your life. You will learn the inside-out approach to personal effectiveness.
Order Code: COVSHHB
Price: $14.00

Leadership is an Art

Max DePree

Max DePree's form of leadership is based on the human values of care and concern. His "wisdom" book teaches how to enrich the sense of personal achievement that is sorely missing in today's workplace. "CEO Max DePree grabs the gold. This book is thoughtful, personal, human, persuasive." - Tom Peters.
Order Code: DEPLAB
Price: $13.00

Leadership Jazz

Max DePree

Max DePree examines excellence in business. By comparing leadership and jazz, DePree shows how a leader can find his or her unique voice while incorporating such conflicting ingredients as freedom and technique, improvisation and rules, inspiration and restraint.
Order Code: DEPLJB
Price: $13.00

DESIGN FIRM | Polivka Logan Design—PLD
ART DIRECTORS/DESIGNERS | Chris Adams, Lisa Noreen
COPYWRITER | Lisa Pemrick
CLIENT | Christian Brother, Inc.
TOOLS | QuarkXPress

This brochure for a manufacturer of hockey sticks helps the clients break into a competitive market with their new product. The piece explains all products and benefits.

CUSTOMIZED
SUPPORT
PROGRAMS

Unique problems bring unique solutions.

You have a professional partner in
CSI Digital, creating custom
solutions to meet your specific
service needs. CSI's technical
support services allow your systems
and your highly skilled staff to
operate at their peak performance
allowing you to do what you do
best — your work.

•CALL 1-800-624-0998 FOR THE OFFICE NEAREST YOU →

Seattle
Portland
San Francisco
Los Angeles
Burbank

TECHNICAL
SERVICES

CSI DIGITAL

DESIGN FIRM | Hornall Anderson Design
Works, Inc.

ART DIRECTOR | John Hornall

DESIGNERS | David Bates, Margaret Long,
John Anicker

CLIENT | CSI Digital

PAPER/PRINTING | Cougar Opaque, Heath
Printers

The client needed a capabilities
brochure that explained the different
technical services of the hardware/
software installation. This brochure
started as a multipurpose brochure that
was integrated into one piece. The client
wanted their technical department to
have its own look, while building on the
piece's overall corporate look.

not just exhibits

DESIGN FIRM | Tanagram
ART DIRECTOR | Eric Wagner
DESIGNER/ILLUSTRATOR | Eric Wagner, David Kaplan, Erik DeBat
COPYWRITER | Lisa Brenner
CLIENT | MG Design
TOOLS | Adobe Photoshop, Macromedia FreeHand, Strata, QuarkXPress
PAPER/PRINTING | Howard Antique Parchment, Productolith/Consolidated Printing

This brochure illustrates the uniquely expansive range of services that
MG Design, an exhibit design company, offers to its clients. The piece is digitally
illustrated and the client's corporate colors were substituted for process colors
on press.

DESIGN FIRM | Sayles Graphic Design

ALL DESIGN | John Sayles

COPYWRITER | Kristin Lennert

CLIENT | Cross America

PAPER/PRINTING | Curtis Tuscan Terracoat/Four-color offset

In developing the new logo for Cross America, a monogram C was incorporated with a globe graphic and complementing typeface. The effect is striking, and the two-color corporate identity is also cost effective. The accompanying brochure features the company's philosophy and services printed on uncoated riblaid paper. The text pages alternate with glossy cast-coated pages featuring dramatic black-and-white photographs of images. The primary focus was to make the piece globally appealing, because of the nature of the client's business.

DESIGN FIRM | Cornoyer-Hedrick, Inc.
ALL DESIGN | Lanie Gotcher
COPYWRITER | Mary Baldwin
CLIENT | Williams Gateway Airport
TOOLS | QuarkXPress, Adobe Illustrator
PAPER | Quintessa 100 lb. dull; Folder/brochure/dividers:
Classic Crest 70 lb.

Designed to transform from a pocket folder to a proposal by trimming
pieces and wirebinding, this piece picks up airport runway elements
and includes a custom pocket folder with information sheets and a
proposal book.

1 DESIGN FIRM | Lee Reedy Design
ART DIRECTOR | Lee Reedy
DESIGNER | Karey Christ-Janer
ILLUSTRATOR | Karey Christ-Janer
PHOTOGRAPHER | Howard Sokol
COPYWRITER | Janet Aitken
CLIENT | Centennial Sedans
PAPER/PRINTER | Lustrocoat, Phoenix Press
TOOLS | QuarkXPress and Adobe Photoshop

2 DESIGN FIRM | Lee Reedy Design
ART DIRECTOR | Lee Reedy
DESIGNERS | Heather Haworth and Kathy Thompson
ILLUSTRATOR | Heather Haworth
CLIENT | National Ski Patrol
PRINTER | Knuntsen Printing, Lange Graphics
TOOL | QuarkXPress

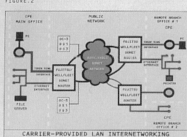

example, a client can fill a spreadsheet on a PC in Chicago with data from a server in Atlanta, and then print the output on a laser printer in Dallas. Businesses are using this kind of company-wide internetworking to give their customers better service.

What's in it for the Public Network Provider?

With the kinds of advantages LAN internetworking can provide, it is no surprise that billions of dollars are spent on it each year. It is an industry that is here today, rather than a market that must wait to become economically feasible. Therefore, a remarkable opportunity exists for the public network providers to capture a larger part of the enormous

revenue spent by businesses using LAN technology.

More of this revenue can be captured for the telcos using the Fujitsu/Wellfleet product because it solves so many problems with internetworking. Better LAN connectivity should result in higher tariffs and more subscribers. Currently, most LANs are connected to private line services via a router or multiplexer that is on the customer's side of the network interface or demarcation point. The telephone company supplies only the T1, leaving the customer to deal with all the protocol compatibility problems, poor throughput, hard-to-provision equipment, and potentially no survivability. Figure 1 is a diagram of the traditional configuration.

The Traditional Internetworking Approach

The LAN office wiring from each PC and peripheral homes into a wiring concentrator. The concentrator in turn has a LAN interface which is connected to another piece of customer equipment, typically a router or a T1 multiplexer. Then, a DS1 interface from the router is connected to a Channel Service Unit (CSU), which finally connects the office to the public network. The connection could also be frame relay, DS3, fractional T1, or digital private line, but the principle is the same. Unfortunately, the customer also has to manage an extensive set of customer premise equipment (CPE) that does not make the wide area network (WAN) transparent to the client.

Problems with Traditional Interworking Become Revenue Opportunities

Customers Do Not Like Managing Complicated CPE Problem: The customer has to purchase and manage the router and CSU. Anyone who has constructed a private network will admit that all the protocols and interface really add up to one big headache. The customer wants to know, "Why can't I just plug my LAN into the wall and

let the telephone company do all the work? I have to have my own staff to administer this stuff. I'd rather spend time making widgets, and let the telco worry about integrating all these technologies."

Solution: Move the CPE into the Public Network. Fujitsu and Wellfleet can provide a combined solution today that gives the business customer a LAN interface rather than a T1, and a hardware solution that works with the FLM 150 ADM (Fujitsu's OC-3/12 SONET multiplexer) and FACTR® (access platform) systems. The integration between Wellfleet's router and Fujitsu's SONET transmission products will evolve over time (as described in AN-94-002), but for now, the two vendors are working together to bring graceful LAN internetworking

to the public network. The telephone company can move the demarcation point further into the customer's premises, all the way to the wiring concentrator. The resulting data service offering translates into a source of new cash flow. Figure 2 shows how the new service could be configured.

The Fujitsu/Wellfleet Approach

As Fujitsu's SONET products work closely with Wellfleet's router, many of the problems of connecting LANs to the network are solved. The SONET/Router functions are being placed into one integrated system that accomplishes LAN connections directly into the SONET network, seamlessly and easily.

The public network provider

With the kinds of advantages LAN internetworking can provide, it is no surprise that billions of dollars are spent on it each year. It is an industry that is here today, rather than a market that must wait to become economically feasible.

DESIGN FIRM | Swieter Design U.S.

ART DIRECTOR | John Swieter

DESIGNER | Mark Ford

CLIENT | Fujitsu-Envoy

TOOLS | QuarkXPress, Adobe Illustrator, and Adobe Photoshop

1

DESIGN FIRM | Greteman Group

ART DIRECTOR | Sonia Greteman

DESIGNERS | Sonia Greteman and James Strange

PHOTOGRAPHER | Larry Fleming

CLIENT | Koch Crime Commission

PRINTER | Donlevey

TOOL | Macromedia FreeHand

1➤ This brochure was used to promote Jesse Jackson's appearance in Wichita. The piece illustrates Jackson's stand on education and crime and depicts students in dramatic photos.

2➤ The objective of this brochure is to compel insurance agents to sell Safeco insurance products and earn incentive points that could add up to a prize-winning cruise.

2

DESIGN FIRM | Gable Design Group

ART DIRECTOR | Tony Gable

DESIGNERS | Tony Gable and Karin Yamagiwa

ILLUSTRATOR | Karin Yamagiwa

COPYWRITER | Safeco Insurance Co.

CLIENT | Safeco Insurance Co.

PRINTER | Heath Printers

TOOL | Adobe PageMaker

DESIGN FIRM | Bernhardt Fudyma Design Group
ART DIRECTOR | Craig Bernhardt
DESIGNER | Janice Fudyma
ILLUSTRATOR | James Yang
COPYWRITER | Jerry Mosier
CLIENT | Hibbard Brown
PRINTER | Quality House of Graphics
TOOL | QuarkXPress

DESIGN FIRM | Marc Marahrens
ART DIRECTOR | Marc Marahrens
DESIGNER | Marc Marahrens
COPYWRITER | Relais & Chateaux
CLIENT | Relais & Chateaux, Deutschland
PRINTER | Format Offset
TOOLS | Macromedia FreeHand and QuarkXPress

The main theme of the brochure is the 5 Cs which is the principle of Relais & Chateaux restaurant and hotel guides.

DESIGN FIRM | Sibley/Peteet
ART DIRECTOR | David Beck
DESIGNER | David Beck
CLIENT | The Image Bank

DESIGN FIRM | Segura Inc.

ART DIRECTOR | Carlos Segura

DESIGNER | Carlos Segura

COPYWRITER | Alan Gandelman

CLIENT | Hart Marx

TOOLS | Adobe Illustrator, QuarkXPress,
and Adobe Photoshop

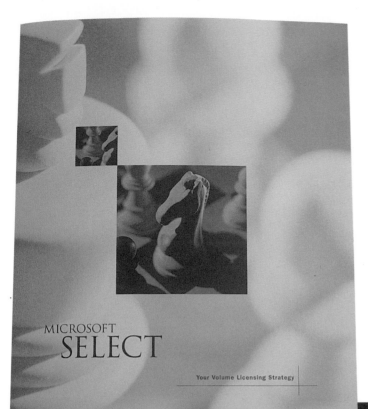

DESIGN FIRM | The Leonhardt Group
DESIGNERS | Tim Young and Jon Cannell
PHOTOGRAPHER | Daniel Langley
COPYWRITER | Tyler Cartier
CLIENT | Microsoft
PAPER/PRINTER | Zanders Ikonofix Matt, United Graphics

REDUCING YOUR RISK OF PIRACY

An Overall View

Copyright law around the world is becoming increasingly more stringent, with severe penalties for software piracy. More than 112 countries are signatories to the General Agreement on Tariffs and Trade (GATT), which provides comprehensive protection of computer software.

The Challenge

It is both difficult and expensive for large organizations to track and audit proper use of software, ensuring compliance with strict copyright laws. Piracy is a major risk and exposure can be disastrous.

Unauthorized software copies lack the strict quality controls built into the original disks, making them far more prone to computer viruses. Viruses put your entire enterprise at risk, including data resources, financial systems and other vital computer functions. The losses go beyond time and money. An organization may never fully recover from negative publicity, diminished credibility and the loss of potential business.

Illegal copies also result in higher prices for upgrades. No technical support is available. And reliability is always suspect. The vast majority of large organizations want to comply with prevailing laws. However, they fear exposure somewhere in their organization because of the difficulty of tracking software acquisition and use.

A Winning Strategy

Legally acquiring software for every machine is the only way to completely protect against illegal copying. Select offers an acquisition option that ensures you own a legal license for every qualifying computer or employee in your organization that's running a particular Microsoft software product.

As an enrollee in the Select program, you will receive quarterly summary reports detailing the total number of purchases you have made to date. That way, you can track what you own without having to do regular spot-checks or internal audits. Select is the most thorough, cost-effective way to ensure complete compliance worldwide — and peace of mind.

DESIGN FIRM | Raven Madd Design

ART DIRECTOR | Mark Curtis

DESIGNER | Mark Curtis

PHOTOGRAPHER | Esther Bunning

CLIENTS | Essence Beauty Therapy, Grace Hair Design,
Partridge Jewellers, Nenarbe Fine Art Photography,
Daisy A Day, Amanda, Nicolle Millinery,
Alison Blain Designer

PRINTER | Neal Print

TOOLS | Macintosh and Macromedia FreeHand

The inserts in this piece are loose, not bound, so
recipients can remove the sections most relevant
to their work.

DESIGN FIRM | Segura Inc.

ART DIRECTOR | Carlos Segura

DESIGNER | Carlos Segura

COPYWRITER | Alan Gandelman

CLIENT | Hart Marx

PRINTER | Argus Press

TOOLS | Adobe Illustrator, QuarkXPress,
 and Adobe Photoshop

MELBOURNE WATER IS ENHANCING THE QUALITY OF LIFE IN WORLD COMMUNITIES BY PROVIDING ENVIRONMENTAL AND ENGINEERING SOLUTIONS THROUGH EXCELLENCE IN CONSULTANCY, TECHNOLOGIES AND OPERATING SERVICES IN THE MANAGEMENT OF **WATER**

DESIGN FIRM | Cato Design Inc.

DESIGNER | Jeff Thornton

CLIENT | Melbourne Water

Designed to promote Melbourne Water to Asian clients, this piece presents the history of Melbourne Water.

1

DESIGN FIRM | Lee Reedy Design
ART DIRECTOR | Lee Reedy
DESIGNER | Lee Reedy
ILLUSTRATOR | Patrick Merewether
COPYWRITER | Lee Reedy
CLIENT | Tumbleweed Press
PAPER/PRINTER | Environment, Tumbleweed Press
TOOL | QuarkXPress

1➤ The dies and colored pencil were scanned into this piece.

2

DESIGN FIRM | Grand Design Co.
ART DIRECTORS | Grand So and Rex Lee
DESIGNER | Rex Lee
ILLUSTRATOR | Rex Lee
COPYWRITER | Finny Maddess Consultants Ltd.
CLIENT | Alchemy Beauty
PRINTER | Goldjoin (Ricky) Printing Co., Ltd.
TOOL | Adobe PageMaker

2

1

DESIGN FIRM | The Criterion Group

ART DIRECTOR | Allison Edwards Cottrill

DESIGNER | Allison Edwards Cottrill

ILLUSTRATOR | Allison Edwards Cottrill

COPYWRITER | Richard Shaw

CLIENT | Rivera Travel Club

TOOL | QuarkXPress

1➤ This piece uses seven colors, and is tinted with varnish. The firm's objective was to create a fun but cleanly designed brochure.

2

DESIGN FIRM | Swieter Design U.S.

ART DIRECTOR | John Swieter

DESIGNERS | John Swieter and Kevin Flatt

ILLUSTRATORS | Jim Vogel and Chris Gall

CLIENT | The Marshall Companies

PRINTER | Williamson Printing

TOOLS | Adobe Illustrator, Adobe Photoshop,
and QuarkXPress

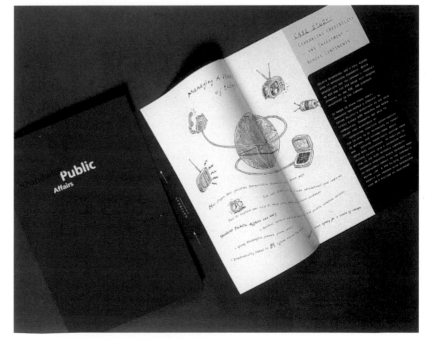

1

DESIGN FIRM | Mires Design

ART DIRECTOR | Scott Mires

DESIGNER | Scott Mires

ILLUSTRATOR | Tracy Sabin

PHOTOGRAPHER | Chris Wimpey

CLIENT | Airtouch Cellular

2

DESIGN FIRM | Prospera

ART DIRECTOR | Karen Geiger

DESIGNERS | Karen Geiger and Bettina Dehuhard

ILLUSTRATOR | Eric Hanson

COPYWRITER | Shandwick Public Affairs

CLIENT | Shandwick Public Affairs

PAPER | Neenah Columns, French Newsprint, Potlatch,
Vintage Velvet

TOOLS | QuarkXPress and Adobe Illustrator

DESIGN FIRM | Carmichael Lynch

ART DIRECTOR | Pete Winecke

DESIGNER | Pete Winecke

PHOTOGRAPHER | Pat Fox Photo

COPYWRITER | Sheldon Glay

CLIENT | Harley-Davidson H.O.G. Division

TOOLS | QuarkXPress and Adobe Photoshop

The challenge here was to design a brochure that reflects a "Harley" way of life.

1

DESIGN FIRM | Studio W. Inc.

ART DIRECTOR | Fo Wilson

DESIGNER | Fo Wilson

PHOTOGRAPHER | Impact Visuals

COPYWRITER | Impact Visuals

CLIENT | Impact Visuals

PAPER/PRINTER | Mohawk, Enterprise Press

TOOLS | QuarkXPress

2

DESIGN FIRM | Sayles Graphic Design

ART DIRECTOR | John Sayles

DESIGNER | John Sayles

ILLUSTRATOR | John Sayles

COPYWRITER | Wendy Lyons

CLIENT | MWR Telecom

PAPER/PRINTER | Curtis Papers, Artcraft Printing

2➤ Designed to promote fiber-optic network services to local businesses, this dictionary-sized piece is made from chip board laminated with paper. The brochure explains the benefits of fiber optics; even in a raging flood, MWR Telecom can transmit the entire dictionary in 1/16 of a second.

DESIGN FIRM | X Design Company

ART DIRECTORS/DESIGNER | Alex Valderrama

CLIENT | McDermott Planning and Design

The goal was to create a brochure that could double as a leave-behind and as a direct mailer. Thus this brochure was designed to stand alone, but it could also be rolled, held together with a belly band, and placed in the box when used for direct mailing.

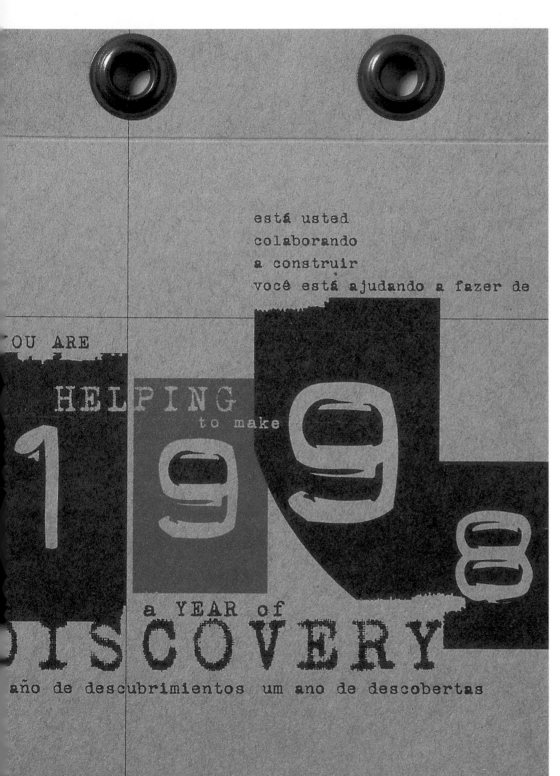

DESIGN FIRM | Pinkhaus Design
ART DIRECTOR | Joel Fuller
DESIGNERS | Cindy Vasquez
COPYWRITER | Doug Paley
CLIENT | Discovery Network
TOOLS | Adobe Illustrator and Photoshop
PAPER | Simpson Evergreen Kraft, 80 lb. cover,
           Champion Pagentry Handmade
PRINTING PROCESS | Four-color process plus two PMS

The client was planning to make a donation in the name of all those who received this Christmas card. The card needed to reflect the significance of this donation and the Spirit of Discovery.

unit control 1.9.9.5. unit control 1.9.9.5.

unit control 1.9.9.5.

Création en mai 1995 à Luxembourg aux Foires Internationales au Kirchberg

Durée: 1H20 Min

Chorégraphie: Bernard Baumgarten

Bernard Baumgarten, chorégraphe luxembourgeois, a débuté sa carrière au S.O.A.P. Dance Theatre à Francfort.

Après des études au Conservatoire de Luxembourg et chez Rick Odums à Paris, il fut engagé comme danseur dans la compagnie de Rui Horta. En 1993, le «Mousonturm» offrait aux membres de la compagnie l'opportunité de produire une soirée chorégraphique. «Im Falle des Fallens eines gefallenen Wortes», chorégraphie de B. Baumgarten, avait suscité l'intérêt par son langage très personnel et ses images, d'une beauté parfois glaciale et distante. Dans ses productions suivantes, «Jedes X Wenn Du», 1994 au Gallus Theater à Francfort, et «Honni soit qui mal y pense», 1994 à l'Atelier Cosmopolite Fondation Royaumont à Paris, il est resté fidèle à son approche chorégraphique, orientée vers l'expression théâtrale de la danse.
Avec unit.control 1. 9. 9. 5. B. Baumgarten franchit une étape importante: les premières pièces ont été chorégraphiées pour 2 à 3 interprètes - la production unit control, créée dans le cadre Luxembourg, Ville Européenne de la Culture, met en scène sept danseurs, un travail vidéographique et la composition d'une musique originale.

Interprètes (performers)
Jacky Achar (F)
Frieder Bachmann (D)
Laurent Cotillard (F)
Cendrine Gallezot (F)
Katrin Pohlmann (D)
Malou Thein (L)
Dirk Vrancken (B)

Musique (music)
Stéphane Broc, Cornelia Francke

Décors et éclairages (set and lighting)
Norbert Mohr

Vidéo (video)
Anna Saup, Cornelia Francke

Animation virtuelle (virtual animation)
Michael Saup

Costumes (costumes)
Inge Zysk

Photos (photographs)
Chris Nash

DESIGN FIRM | Atelier Graphique Bizart
ART DIRECTOR | Raoul Thill
DESIGNER | Miriam Rosner
PHOTOGRAPHERS | Katrin Schander, Chris Nash
COPYWRITER | Stephane Broc
CLIENT | Theâtre Dansé & Muet
TOOLS | Adobe Photoshop, QuarkXPress
PAPER | Zanders Megamatt
PRINTING PROCESS | Black and silver offset

The client was very open to a free style of graphic design. Being able to break typographical rules was helpful in depicting movement, dynamism, and the way dancers expresses themselves.

DESIGN FIRM | Melissa Passehl Design
ALL DESIGN | Melissa Passehl
CLIENT | Interchange Family Services
TOOLS | QuarkXPress, Adobe Illustrator and Photoshop
PAPER | Lustro Dull
PRINTING PROCESS | Four-color lithography

This brochure is a quick reference for families with special-needs children aged one to three. Color and hand-rendered type help to create a child-friendly feeling.

the goal of Interchange is to promote appropriate and coordinated services for families and their infants and toddlers who have special needs or are at risk of developmental delays.

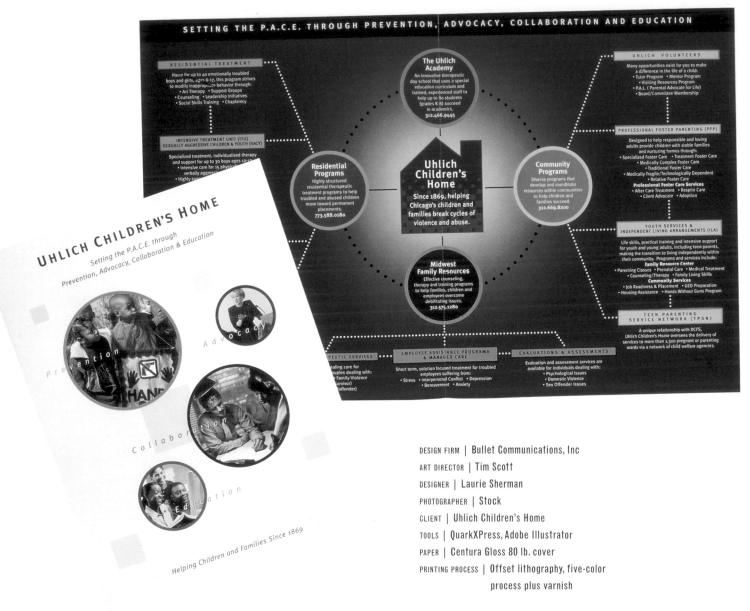

DESIGN FIRM | Bullet Communications, Inc

ART DIRECTOR | Tim Scott

DESIGNER | Laurie Sherman

PHOTOGRAPHER | Stock

CLIENT | Uhlich Children's Home

TOOLS | QuarkXPress, Adobe Illustrator

PAPER | Centura Gloss 80 lb. cover

PRINTING PROCESS | Offset lithography, five-color
process plus varnish

This brochure illustrates how Uhlich Children's Home
is Setting the P.A.C.E. in the social-services industry
through its full array of programs and services.

AUSTRALIAN DESIGN

nineteen
98
MCMXCVIII

awards

the search for excellence

call for entries.

DESIGN FIRM | Elton Ward Design

ART DIRECTOR | Jason Moore

DESIGNER | Justin Young

CLIENT | Australian Design Awards

TOOLS | Adobe Illustrator and Photoshop

PAPER | 350 gsm A2 Gloss Art

PRINTING PROCESS | Four-color offset plus special
plus varnish

A technical approach was required for this call-for-entries leaflet to encourage industrial designers to submit their product designs for judging in the 1998 awards competition. This brochure set the theme for the upcoming award-winners annual.

Using dramatic color and photography, the brochure repositions an older, mid-sized flavor-and-fragrance formulator as Master of the Elements. The idea was to create a visual experience of history, color, and capability. The transformation photo illustrates this idea.

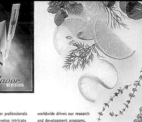

Creating just the right fragrance takes more than science; it also takes the flair, creativity and instinct of our expert perfumers. This combination has helped Ungerer create truly inspirational fragrances.

We work with each client individually to create precisely the right fragrance to meet specific needs.

We test the fragrance in its base for compatibility, efficiency, stability and cost effectiveness. Then, we conduct market tests to ensure consumer acceptance. This painstaking process creates new ideas and fragrances that help distinguish our clients' brands and product lines.

Clients can also opt to choose from the extensive Ungerer database of fragrances for applications ranging from household and industrial products to toiletries and fine fragrances. This database is constantly updated to ensure we have a comprehensive range of fully tested compounds readily available.

We also anticipate trends, constantly focusing on what's "in vogue" with consumers. We evaluate current product lines to determine what's missing and suggest new product line extensions. This close working relationship with customers has become an integral part of the Ungerer culture and helps to create the synergy needed for a successful end product.

Whether a client chooses a custom-created fragrance, or one from our library, we guarantee it to be of the highest quality.

Ungerer's flavor professionals design and develop intricate and complex flavors using essential oils, aromatic chemicals, specialty products, essences, distillates and raw materials acquired throughout the world. We believe that partnership with our customers is the key to serving their needs.

Our experienced flavorists and food technologists in the United States and our plants overseas develop new applications for current products and advise on new product ideas and formulations.

We pride ourselves on responding with the most innovative blends, forever pushing back the barriers of authenticity and naturalness. Keeping abreast of what is happening in the marketplace worldwide drives our research and development programs. We understand the value of investing today in technology needed to produce the flavors of tomorrow. Our flavorists and food technologists work closely together, pooling their creativity and knowledge.

Clients can choose a custom-designed flavor or one from our flavor library. We believe in creating a "win-win" situation for Ungerer and its customers, and to this end, we bring our customers the highest level of creativity, technical innovation, service and quality available.

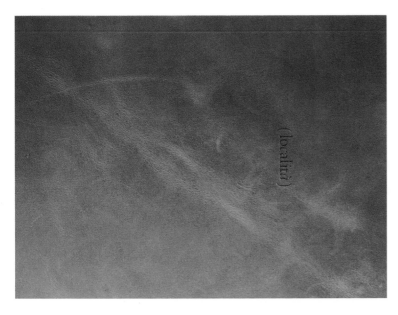

< 18
19
20

DESIGN FIRM | Wood Design

ART DIRECTOR | Tom Wood

DESIGNERS | Tom Wood, Alyssa Weinstein

PHOTOGRAPHER | Craig Cutler

CLIENT | Craig Cutler Photography

TOOLS | QuarkXPress

PAPER | Monadnock Astrolite

PRINTING PROCESS | Six-color offset

The photographer, recognized as a leading studio photographer, requested a promotion that would show his other photographic talents in portrait and location work. The designers played on the concept of travel and places. They paralleled and contrasted the photography in a leatherette-style passport book.

DESIGN FIRM | Price Learman Associates

ART DIRECTOR | Patricia Price Learman

DESIGNER | Sandy Goranson

COPYWRITER | Douglas Learman

CLIENT | Trammell Crow Residential Services;
Chandler's Reach

PAPER | Starwhite Vicksburg Archiva cover and text;
UV Ultra 36 lb. flysheet

PRINTING PROCESS | Four-color process

The client wanted to enhance the Chandler's Reach image, gain upscale residents, and portray an overall feeling of uniqueness. The brochure has the hint of a posh boathouse atmosphere with views of the property's lake activity and the rope that ties it all together.

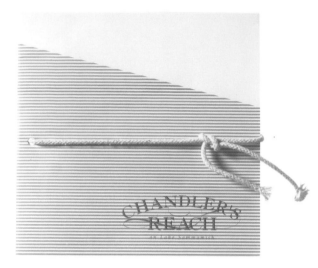

TRAIN for **Change**

...IONS: Rooms have been reserved at the *Holiday Inn,* ...entucky for the nights of *August 24, 25, and 26.* ...rate for TRAIN FOR CHANGE is *$75.00 plus tax.* ...the Holiday Inn directly at *606.331.1500* to ...please indicate that you are attending the ...rkshop when making your reservation. ...e that our special rate is reserved only until *July 30, 1998.* ...our convenience, the Holiday Inn offers a complimentary shuttle ...the airport. We will send you more information about the hotel ...es, including a map, in your enrollment confirmation packet.

...RATION DEADLINE: Your registration must be postmarked on or ...*July 24, 1998,* to guarantee your spot at TRAIN FOR CHANGE.

...ESTIONS? If you have questions about TRAIN FOR CHANGE or ...eed any assistance, please call JULIE HILE or CAROL HOENIGES at THE TRAINING CONNECTION at *309.454.2218.*

TRAIN FOR CHANGE – AUGUST 25, 26, AND 27, 1998
THE TRAINING CONNECTION

DESIGN FIRM | Griffin Design
DESIGNER/ILLUSTRATOR | Tracy Sleeter
COPYWRITER | Carol Hoeniges
CLIENT | The Training Connection
PAPER | Neenah Peppered Bronze Duplex
      Classic Laid (folder)
PRINTING PROCESS | Two-color offset by Commercial Printing
      Associates (folder and inserts);
      four-color Indigo by Starnet (stickers)

The goal was to produce a multi-functional marketing tool. The self-mailing folder, printed with two colors on the inside only, can be used to hold conference promotions or marketing information. An indigo press was used to create multiple sets of stickers that provide artwork on the outside of the folder.

DESIGN FIRM | Adele Bass & Co. Design

ALL DESIGN | Adele Bass

COPYWRITER | Tina Gordon-McBee

CLIENT | Social Model Recovery Systems

TOOLS | Adobe Illustrator and Photoshop, QuarkXPress

PAPER | Evergreen 80-lb., Kraft Cover

PRINTING PROCESS | One-color lithography

Budget was a major consideration for this pamphlet.
The theme of violence inspired the typography on the
cover and the inside copy. The Kraft paper adds to the
raw nature of the subject matter.

operation BWM

BRENTWOOD MALL

no. 1998   military documents inside

IT'S WAR

on our competitors.

ANNUAL GENERAL MEETING
Handout Information

1ST on the agenda   04.21.98

1. Welcome and Call to Order
2. Opening Remarks and President's Message
3. Centre Manager's Comments
4. Approval of Minutes from 1997 AGM
5. Auditor's Report and Financial Statements
6. Appointment of Auditor
7. Election of 1998/99 Board of Directors
8. Marketing Director's Report
9. Election Results
10. 1997 Merchant Achievement Awards
11. Prize Draw
12. Guest Speaker: Dan Charrette, Statistics Canada
13. New Business
14. Adjournment

Divine Dividends a Heavenly STIR

Brentwood Mall launched our Divine Dividends Customer Rewards Program in 1997 with the intent to encourage Brentwood customers to shop more frequently, increase individual expenditures per visit and encourage these goals throughout the year. The incentive was a collectible series of custom-designed Angels created exclusively for Brentwood Mall. Advertised within the shopping centre only, the program boasted over 600 members and represented over $98,000.00 in sales revenue.

Winner of MERIT Maple Leaf Award: Overall Marketing Campaign

This award recognizes a single campaign that combines elements from at least two areas of shopping centre marketing. The category looks for synergy of well-integrated marketing programs that use multiple and varied efforts to benefit their shopping centres. Our 'Make the Season Bright' Christmas campaign integrated sales promotion, consumer advertising, customer relations and community program initiatives to give customers unique reasons to shop at Brentwood Mall.

1997 HIGHLIGHTS

special EVENTS for 1998

ITEMS TO REMEMBER
SO YOU CAN PLAN AHEAD

Youth Week: May	Antique Show: September
Antique Show: May	Halloween Festivities: October
Safety Week: June	Christmas Promotions:
Sidewalk Sale: July	November/December
Back To School Promotion:	Sidewalk Sale:
August/September	January 1999

DESIGN FIRM | Big Eye Creative, Inc.
ALL DESIGN | Nancy Yeasting
COPYWRITERS | Nancy Yeasting, Folanda Smits
CLIENT | Brentwood Mall
TOOLS | Adobe Illustrator and Photoshop
PAPER | Currency Cover Silver and blueprint paper
PRINTING PROCESS | Lithography and blueprints

This annual meeting for a local mall required economical print material to promote their war against the retail

Great Valley Center

LEGACI Grants

DESIGN FIRM | Shields Design
ART DIRECTOR/DESIGNER | Charles Shields
PHOTOGRAPHER | Stock
COPYWRITER | Carol Whiteside
CLIENT | Great Valley Center
TOOLS | Adobe Illustrator and Photoshop
PAPER | Classic Crest 70 lb. text
PRINTING PROCESS | Offset

This was an inexpensive, two-color brochure for a local client. It combines information about available grants and an application form. Within a limited budget, the client wanted a sophisticated brochure to showcase the new program.

DESIGN FIRM | X Design Company

ART DIRECTOR/DESIGNER | Alex Valderrama

CLIENT | Northwest Bank

TOOLS | QuarkXPress, Adobe Photoshop

PAPER | Cougar Opaque, Beckett RSVP

PRINTING PROCESS | Cougar Opaque, Beckett RSVP

The challenge was to design an invitation that did not look like a direct-mail piece. The solution drew inspiration from researching visuals of China. He treated the invitation like packaging and established a creative visual language. Client expected 1,200 responses and received double that.

We're taking off the gloves on this one! Yes, we've given away cars before, but never like this. Steer your customers in the right direction and your sales will shift into high gear. So will your chances to win! You're in the driver's seat and the race to the finish is in your hands.

WE'LL STEER you

TURN ON THE POWER

WIN A CAR

RIGHT!

DESIGN FIRM | Vaughn Wedeen Creative
ART DIRECTOR | Steve Weeden
DESIGNERS | Steve Weeden, Pam Farrington
COPYWRITER | Foster Hurley
CLIENT | US West

DESIGN FIRM | Black Cat Design
ART DIRECTORS | Anthony Secolo, Kelly Coller
DESIGNER/ILLUSTRATOR | Anthony Secolo
COPYWRITER | Kelly Coller
CLIENT | Seattle Opera's Bravo! Club
TOOLS | Macromedia FreeHand, Adobe Photoshop
PAPER | Fox River White
PRINTING PROCESS | One-color plus varnish

Varnish worked beautifully in this brochure,
lending rich color.

DESIGN FIRM | Wood Design & Art Studio

ART DIRECTOR/DESIGNER | Linda Wood

COPYWRITER | Doreen Lecheler, Project C.U.R.E.

CLIENT | Project C.U.R.E

TOOLS | QuarkXPress, Adobe Photoshop

PAPER | Grafika Vellum—Autumn Mist

PRINTING PROCESS | One-color offset

The Pasaporté's key visual feature is the passport-style leather pocket created to simulate a quarterly invitation for armchair travel to featured countries. Project C.U.R.E. collects and donates surplus medical supplies to Third World countries.

Pasaporté to North KOREA

Editor
Doreen M. Lecheler

Contributing Editor
Erin E. Jackson

Graphic Design
Wood Design & Art Studio
Linda Wood

President
Dr. W. Douglas Jackson

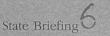

PASAPORTÉ to North Korea
Spring 1998
Volume 1, Number 1 1.1

PASAPORTÉ is a quarterly publication of Project C.U.R.E. If you know someone who would like to receive a free subscription to PASAPORTÉ, please call (303) 727-9414. Please send address corrections to the address below. Copyright © 1998. Permission to reprint in whole or in part is hereby granted, provided a copy of the reprinted article is sent to Project C.U.R.E. and a version of the following credit line is included: "Reprinted by permission from PASAPORTÉ, the quarterly journal of Project C.U.R.E."

Project C.U.R.E.
2040 South Navajo
Denver, Colorado
80223-3848

Phone
303.727.9414

Fax
303.727.8397

projectcure@juno.com

North Korea
a view from inside
by
James W. Jackson

The Palace of Gifts, housing treasures given to Kim Il Sung by other world leaders (1995)

James W. Jackson is a successful businessman, author, international economic consultant and humanitarian. Jackson has served as economic consultant to various governments and businesses. He received the Gold Medallion Book Award in recognition of his works. He is the founder, chairman of the board and past president of the Benevolent Brotherhood Foundation, Inc. For the past 10 years, Jackson has volunteered full-time to direct Project C.U.R.E. To date he has consulted with heads of governments and health officials in 58 countries, including DPRK, China, Cuba and the former Soviet countries.

Jackson was the first person to receive State Department clearance and licensing for shipping to DPRK and Cuba. His work with foreign officials has awarded him many national and international honors, including "Who's Who in Business" and "International Man of the Year" in 1991.

A HISTORY OF RISK

Since 1950 the Democratic People's Republic of Korea (North Korea) was one of the most adamant Communist players in the Cold War stalemate. The country, with its socialist leader Great Leader Kim Il Sung, was seen as the most natural and least expensive safeguard for protecting the back door of Russia and China. Following the Korean War, Joseph Stalin and Mao Tse-tung determined to subsidize the government and army of Kim Il Sung for the purpose of defense against the United States and Republic of Korea troops stationed south of the 38th Parallel. It was more efficient to pay for Kim's efforts than to deploy Soviet or Chinese armies to guard the borders.

The strategy toward D.P.R.K. has been quite simple and very consistent: one of deterrence through a strong military defense. Throughout the years, there has been a legitimate threat of rekindled aggression. Many times both sides have been totally convinced that out-and-out war would again commence as a result of some overt provocation from one camp or the other, e.g. the South's Francis Gary Powers situation, the Pueblo occurrence, the North's bombing of the South Korea Airline KAL flight #858 in 1987 or the recent submarine grounding on the South Korean coast.

This risk management strategy has worked well to bring relative stability to the Korean peninsula. Neither the North nor the South has engaged in any type of preemptive strike. However, the strategy of deterrence has come at a very high price. For South Korea, the price has been approximately $15 billion per year for military defense. The U.S. spends more than $3 billion per year to support some 37,000 troops in

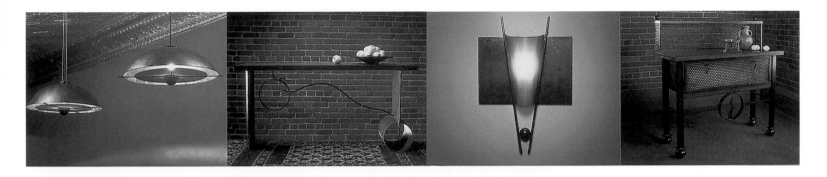

ROCK 'N' Steel

DESIGN FIRM | Greteman Group
ART DIRECTOR | Sonia Greteman
DESIGNERS | Craig Tomson, Sonia Greteman
PHOTOGRAPHER | Steve Rasmussen
COPYWRITER | Deanna Harms
CLIENT | Rock-n-Steel
TOOLS | Macromedia FreeHand, Adobe Photoshop
PAPER | Reflections
PRINTING PROCESS | Four-color process

In spite of a low budget, this four-color, accordion-fold brochure does its job. Its postcard-sized photographs showcase samples of the firm's work in sculpture, metal, stone, and wood.

INSTITUTIONAL
BROCHURES

DESIGN FIRM | Insight Design Communications
ART DIRECTORS | Tracy and Sherrie Holdeman
DESIGNER | Chris Parks
CLIENT | Comcare
TOOLS | Macromedia FreeHand, Adobe Photoshop

Mental-health professionals use art therapy as one of their tools in treating patients. This annual report incorporates actual art therapy illustrations and the treatment goals these illustrations represent to exemplify the services of the individual departments.

Why

invest or rent in

London?

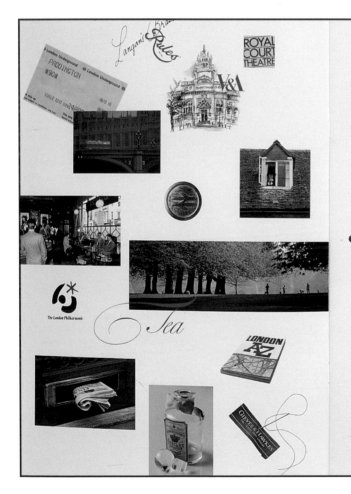

...because

London is one of the truly great cities of the world with green parklands, wide open spaces, palaces, elegant houses, museums, theatres and attractive shops. It is also safe in the broadest sense of personal security and offers comprehensive facilities for recreation and educational pursuits. London is one of the leading business centres of the world and is an important centre of communications between Asia and America.

Historically, it has made good financial sense for Britons living abroad as expatriates to maintain a stake in the UK property market through a residential property investment in London. For residents of the United Kingdom, the inclusion of a well-managed property investment in the Capital can be financially rewarding and, for non-British individuals, a combination of the soundness of the British constitutional system and a stable market provides a safe environment in which to

invest with confidence.

DESIGN FIRM | George Tscherny

ART DIRECTOR | George Tscherny

DESIGNERS | George Tscherny and Lynne Buchman

COPYWRITER | Chris Dick

CLIENT | PKL Limited

PAPER/PRINTER | Parilux, Matte White, 127 lb. Balding and Mansell (England)

PKL Limited sells and rents real estate in London. The designers' premise in creating the brochure was that they had to sell London before selling the company. The result was a cover that teased the reader into turning the page for an answer to the question.

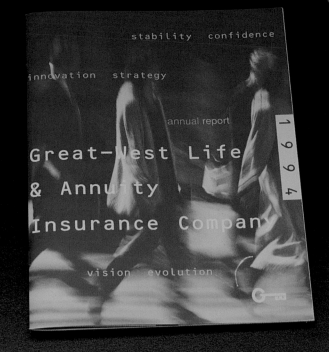

DESIGN FIRM | Lee Reedy Design

ART DIRECTOR | Lee Reedy

DESIGNER | Heather Haworth

ILLUSTRATOR | Heather Haworth

PHOTOGRAPHER | Ron Coppock and stock

COPYWRITER | Great West

CLIENT | Great West

PAPER/PRINTER | Productolith, L & M Printing

TOOLS | QuarkXPress, Adobe Illustrator, Macromedia
FreeHand, and Adobe Photoshop

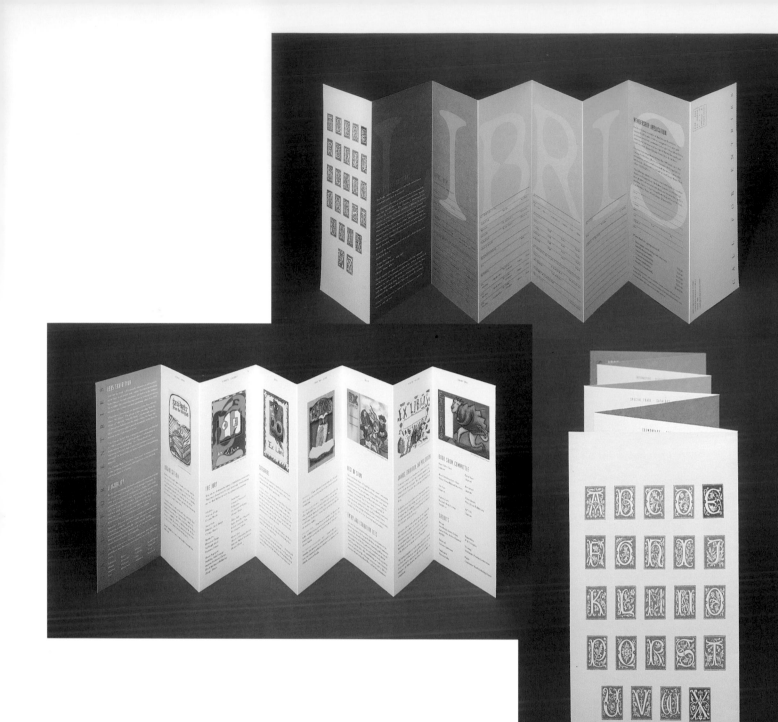

DESIGN FIRM | Ligature, Inc.

ART DIRECTOR | Jeff Wills

DESIGNERS | John Menefee, Tamra Nelson,
Jundine O'Shea, and Kristen Perantoni

ILLUSTRATORS | Chuck Gonzales, Jose Ortega,
Victoria Raymond, Susan Swan, Latjana Krizmanic,
Leslie Cober-Gentry, and Marie Lafrance

COPYWRITER | Adrienne Lieberman

CLIENT | The Chicago Book Clinic

PAPER/PRINTER | Scott Vellum Opaque Cover, 65 lb, Cream,
Wicklander Printing Corporation

TOOLS | QuarkXPress and Adobe Photoshop

The Chicago Book Clinic is a nonprofit organization.
The artists and suppliers who worked on this project donated their time, services, and goods. The
designers chose the Ex Libris, or bookplate theme, in
the tradition of fine book making. Each illustration
is a bookplate which represents a different entry
category.

DESIGN FIRM | Sayles Graphic Design

ART DIRECTOR | John Sayles

DESIGNER | John Sayles

ILLUSTRATOR | John Sayles

COPYWRITER | Wendy Lyons

CLIENT | Drake University

PAPER/PRINTER | Curtis Tuscan Antique, Action Print, Acme Printing

For this fraternity/sorority "rush" recruitment mailing, the designer used found objects, including paper remnants from a recently completed corporate project, scrap corrugated cardboard, and industrial office supply materials. Perhaps the most innovative material found is the front cover of the piece; it is an actual metal printing plate. Although they were never actually used in the printing process, the plates have been burned with the project title "Greek Life: Get A Feel For It."

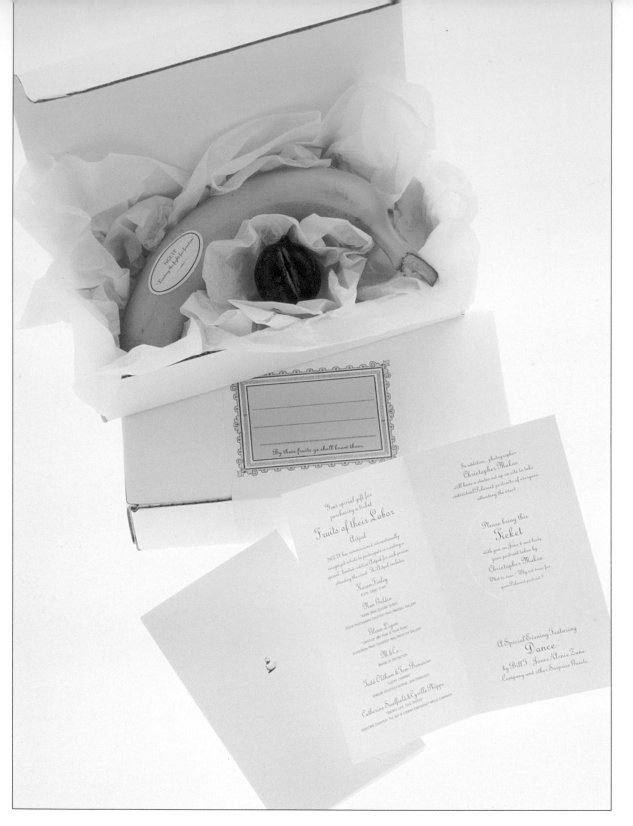

DESIGN FIRM | M & Company

ART DIRECTOR | Stefan Sagmeister

DESIGNER | Stefan Sagmeister and Tom Walker

ILLUSTRATOR | Tom Walker

COPYWRITERS | Lee Brown and Stefan Sagmeister

CLIENT | Gay and Lesbian Task Force

PAPER/PRINTER | 80 lb. uncoated corrugated box, tissue paper

This brochure comes in a box with a real banana and plum. Two thousand pieces were sent out during a summer heat wave, making production a nightmare. The bananas were rotten by the time the plums arrived, but in the end, the project was a success. Most of the packages were hand-delivered.

Girl Scouts Of
Santa Clara County
Annual Report
1993~1994

THE
Faces
OF GIRL SCOUTING

2   1

DESIGN FIRM | Melissa Passehl Design

ART DIRECTOR | Melissa Passehl

DESIGNERS | Melissa Passehl and Jill Steinfeld

ILLUSTRATOR | Betty Bates

PHOTOGRAPHER | Franklin Avery

COPYWRITER | Susan Sharpe

CLIENT | Girl Scouts of Santa Clara County

PAPER/PRINTER | Simpson Quest Auburn 80 lb. cover, Karma
100 lb. text, Meitzler Printing

1➤ With "The Faces Of Girl Scouting" in mind, this
annual report represents the multi-cultural diversity and empowering programs that are characteristic of the Girl Scouts. The illustrations and photographs create a playful solution within this small,
spiral-bound format.

2

DESIGN FIRM | Segura Inc, USA Partners

ART DIRECTORS | Carlos Segura, Dana Arnett, and Ken Fox

DESIGNER | Carlos Segura

COPYWRITER | USA Partners

CLIENT | Harley-Davidson

TOOLS | Adobe Illustrator, QuarkXPress, Adobe Photoshop

1

DESIGN FIRM | Richard Endly Design, Inc.

ART DIRECTOR | Bob Berken

DESIGNER | Keith Wolf

CLIENT | Business Incentives, Motorola

TOOLS | Adobe Illustrator, Adobe Photoshop,
and QuarkXPress

2

DESIGN FIRM | Caldera Design

ART DIRECTOR | Paul Caldera

DESIGNERS | Tim Fisher and Paul Caldera

ILLUSTRATOR | Jacques Barbey

CLIENT | Phelps Dodge

TOOLS | QuarkXPress and Adobe Photoshop

2➤ Caldera Design used a combination of electronic
and live photos to create the composite of images
on the inside of the brochure.

PHELPS DODGE CORPORATION

CANDELARIA

SX/EW

CARBON BLACKS

1994 ANNUAL REPORT

25

PHELPS DODGE INDUSTRIES

Phelps Dodge Industries will use strategic acquisitions, modernization, expansion, new product development and technological leadership to strive to double its 1992 operating cash flow by the end of the century. The companies of Phelps Dodge Industries possess significant market shares, internationally competitive costs, and the commitment of their 9,000 employees to quality and customer partnerships.

Phelps Dodge Industries consists of leading companies and their associate companies that produce wheels and rims for medium and heavy trucks, trailers and buses; carbon blacks and synthetic iron oxides; magnet wire, electrical and telecommunications cables; and specialty high performance conductors. The core companies of Phelps Dodge Industries are Accuride Corporation, Columbian Chemicals Company, Phelps Dodge International Corporation, Phelps Dodge Magnet Wire Company and Hudson International Conductors.

1994 RESULTS

In 1994, Phelps Dodge Industries recorded operating income of $150.7 million, which was reduced to $106.1 million by $44.6 million of non-recurring pre-tax charges applicable to its operations. Phelps Dodge Industries reported record revenues of $1.47 billion with increased annual earnings reflecting higher 1994 sales volumes in the wheel and rim business, the magnet wire business and the carbon black business. Phelps Dodge Industries made $55.1 million in capital expenditures in 1994. Recent modernizations, expansions and acquisitions enabled these businesses to capitalize on the strong North American economy.

In 1994, eight operating facilities and a research laboratory of Phelps Dodge Industries received ISO certification in recognition of the quality systems standards formulated for manufacturing companies worldwide by the prestigious International Organization of Standardization. This brings the total number of ISO quality certifications obtained by Phelps Dodge Industries to 19.

For the second consecutive year, three associate companies of Phelps Dodge International Corporation received the 1994 *Phelps Dodge Corporation Chairman's International Safety Award.*

Columbian Chemicals Company

Phelps Dodge International Corporation

Hudson International Conductors

Phelps Dodge Magnet Wire Company

Accuride Corporation

DESIGN FIRM | Kan Tai-keung Design & Associates Ltd.

ART DIRECTORS | Kan Tai-keung, Freeman Lau Siu Hong,
and Clement Yick Tat Wa

DESIGNERS | Clement Yick Tat Wa and Joyce Ho Ngai Sing

PHOTOGRAPHER | C K Wong

CLIENT | Manhattan Card Co. Ltd.

PAPER/PRINTER | Coated Art Paper, Elegance
Printing Co. Ltd.

TOOLS | Adobe Photoshop and Macromedia FreeHand

DESIGN FIRM | The Design Group
ART DIRECTOR | Stefan Sagmeister
DESIGNERS | Stefan Sagmeister, Peter Rae,
  and Patrick Daily
COPYWRITER | Stefan Sagmeister
CLIENT | Leo Burnett Hong Kong

The Design Group created this piece for a creative conference. To make it interesting, they found out the eye color of every participant, had glass eyes manufactured to spec and placed them in a die cut in the notebook. Then they bound the notebooks by hand.

DESIGNERS | Kimberly Cooke and Ann Freerks
PHOTOGRAPHER | Jon Van Allen
COPYWRITER | Kimberly Cooke
CLIENT | The Visual Arts Alliance
PAPER/PRINTER | Simpson Kashmir,
 Goodfellow Printing, Inc.
TOOLS | Adobe PageMaker

The Visual Arts Alliance is a non-profit organization.
All services that went into creating their recruitment
brochure were donated.

DESIGN FIRM | Wehrman & Company, Inc.

ART DIRECTOR | Ken Wehrman

DESIGNER | Greg Jager

ILLUSTRATOR | Greg Jager

PHOTOGRAPHER | Gretchen Poag

COPYWRITER | Mary Bufe

CLIENT | Insituform Mid-America

PAPER/PRINTER | Glen Eagle Dull,
Reprox Commercial Printing

TOOL | Adobe Photoshop

High-resolution Photoshop montages show the diversity
of Insituform Mid-America technologies.

DESIGN FIRM | Metropolis Corporation
ART DIRECTOR | Denise Mendelsohn
DESIGNER | Lisa Deseno
ILLUSTRATOR | Warren Gerbert
CLIENT | Booz, Allen & Hamilton
PRINTER | W. Mac Printing

DESIGN FIRM | Mires Design
ART DIRECTOR | John Ball
DESIGNERS | John Ball and Gale Spitzley
CLIENT | California Center For The Arts Museum
TOOLS | QuarkXPress and Adobe Illustrator

1

DESIGN FIRM | Lee Reedy Design

ART DIRECTOR | Lee Reedy

DESIGNERS | Lee Reedy and Heather Haworth

ILLUSTRATOR | Heather Haworth

PHOTOGRAPHER | Ken Bisio

COPYWRITER | Marilyn Starrett

CLIENT | Kaiser Permanente

PAPER/PRINTER | Lithofect, Frederic Printing

TOOL | QuarkXPress

2

DESIGN FIRM | Mires Design

ART DIRECTOR | John Ball

DESIGNERS | John Ball and Miguel Perez

ILLUSTRATOR | Tracy Sabin

PHOTOGRAPHER | Carl Vanderschult

CLIENT | California Center For The Arts, Escondido

TOOLS | QuarkXPress and Adobe Illustrator

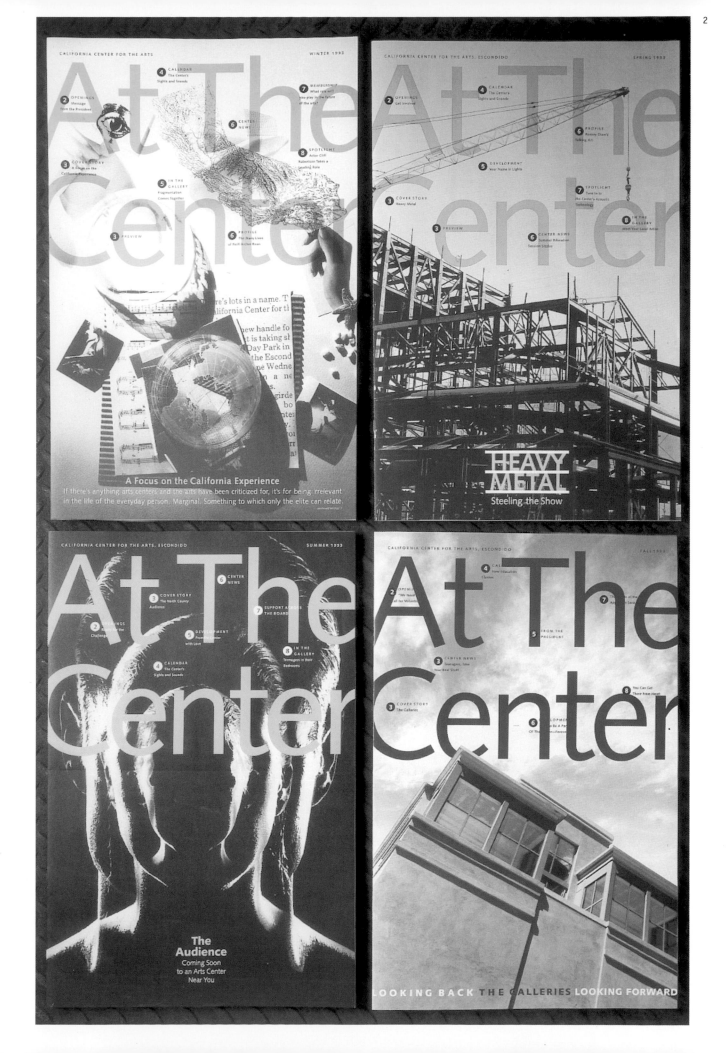

DESIGN FIRM | Morgan Design Studio, Inc.

ART DIRECTOR | Michael Morgan

DESIGNER | Kevin Fitzgerald

PHOTOGRAPHER | Kara Brennan

CLIENT | Atlanta Community Food Bank

TOOLS | QuarkXPress

PAPER | Coated on two sides

PRINTING PROCESS | Four-color process

The client wanted a marketing campaign that would inspire families and people of all ages to join the Hunger Walk. The design team used four different photos to promote the event and to entice viewers to look, read, and participate.

THE ENTERTAINMENT INDUSTRY

EXPANDS

1998 ELECTRONIC ARTS ANNUAL REPORT

DESIGN FIRM | The Leonhardt Group
DESIGNERS | Ray Ueno, Jon Cannell
PHOTOGRAPHERS | Jim Linna Photography,
　　　　　　　　　Jonathan Daniel—1994 World Cup Crowd
CLIENT | Electronic Arts

Firmly in the driver's seat of interactive entertainment, Electronic Arts continues to expand and redefine its own industry. EA is now the world's top-selling publisher of interactive entertainment software. The Leonhart Group felt "expansion was a natural theme for EA in 1998."

HOME BY THE SEA
the development of Newburyport's residential architecture

with Bernard L. Herman

APRIL 25th
SATURDAY
8:30 - 5:00

ARCHITECTURALLY SPEAKING
The Architectural Heritage Program of the Historical Society of Old Newbury

DESIGN FIRM | Johnson Graphics
ART DIRECTOR/DESIGNER | Irene Johnson
ILLUSTRATOR | Richard W. Johnson
COPYWRITER | Adair Rowland
CLIENT | Historical Society of Old Newbury
TOOLS | QuarkXPress, Adobe Photoshop
PAPER | Desert Storm
PRINTING PROCESS | One-color, black with screen

Johnson Graphics created a single-use, economical self-mailer advertising a seminar on historic homes. The period architectural element placed over an old floor plan on Kraft paper imparts the antique feeling the client desired.

"Now that we have this expertise, staff and training, how do we meet new clients?"

"How do we find a firm with the expertise for our project?"

DESIGN FIRM | Michael Courtney Design
ART DIRECTOR/DESIGNER | Michael Courtney
PHOTOGRAPHER | Stock
COPYWRITERS | Susan Ruby, SMDS team
CLIENT | Society for Marketing Professionals,
Seattle chapter
TOOLS | Macromedia FreeHand, Adobe Photoshop
PRINTING PROCESS | Duotone

The objective was to design a distinctive announcement to draw a design literate group (marketing directors) to a professional seminar. The solution was to create an oversized piece with distinctive colors, stock photography, and a tickler reminder card.

Crafts National 30 Juried Exhibition *Call For Entries*

1996 CENTRAL PENNSYLVANIA FESTIVAL OF THE ARTS

DESIGN FIRM | Sommese Design

ART DIRECTOR/ILLUSTRATOR | Lanny Sommese

DESIGNER | Marina Garza

COPYWRITER | Phil Walz

CLIENT | Central Pennsylvania Festival of the Arts

TOOLS | QuarkXPress

PAPER | Cross Point Genesis

PRINTING PROCESS | Offset lithography

The brochures needed to be individualized while retaining a consistent look that was harmonious with the graphics of the arts festival.

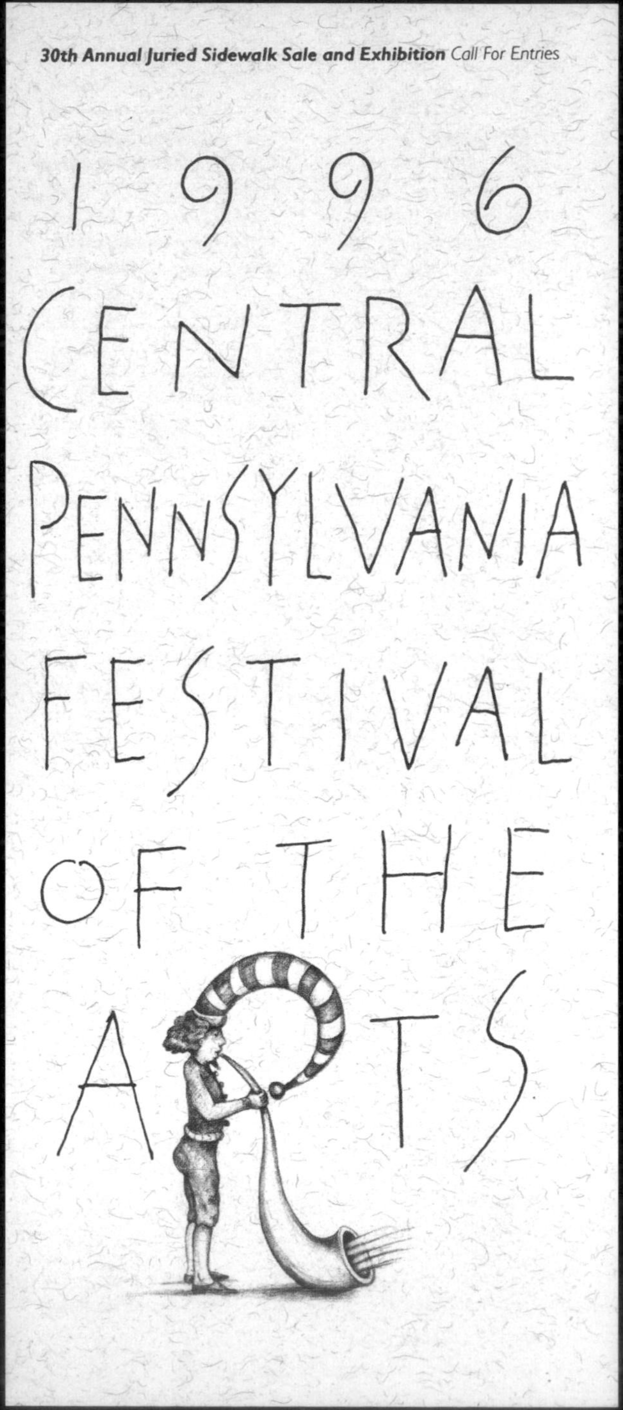

30th Annual Juried Sidewalk Sale and Exhibition *Call For Entries*

1996 CENTRAL PENNSYLVANIA FESTIVAL OF THE ARTS

DESIGN FIRM | Joseph Rattan Design

ART DIRECTOR | Joe Rattan

DESIGNERS | Joe Rattan, Brandon Murphy

ILLUSTRATOR | Michael Crampton

CLIENT | Dallas Children's Theatre

PAPER | Starwhite

PRINTING PROCESS | Offset

This is a vehicle for the marketing communications firm
to announce its name change and to provide its clients
with a taste of its marketing and branding philosophies,
in a format that commands attention.

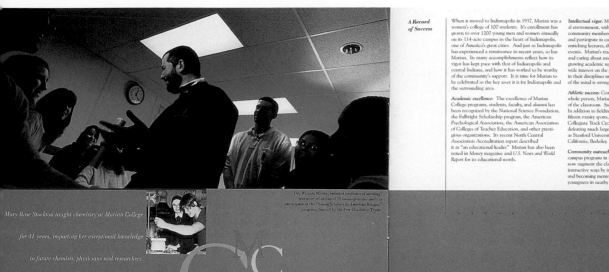

When it moved to Indianapolis in 1937, Marian was a women's college of 100 students. It's enrollment has grown to over 1200 young men and women annually on its 114-acre campus in the heart of Indianapolis, one of America's great cities. And just as Indianapolis has experienced a renaissance in recent years, so has Marian. Its many accomplishments reflect how its vigor has kept pace with that of Indianapolis and central Indiana, and how it has worked to be worthy of the community's support. It is time for Marian to be celebrated as the key asset it is for Indianapolis and the surrounding area.

Academic excellence: The excellence of Marian College programs, students, faculty, and alumni has been recognized by the National Science Foundation, the Fulbright Scholarship program, the American Psychological Association, the American Association of Colleges of Teacher Education, and other prestigious organizations. Its recent North Central Association Accreditation report described it as "an educational leader." Marian has also been noted in *Money* magazine and *U.S. News and World Report* for its educational worth.

Intellectual vigor: Marian promotes a lively intellectual environment, with students, faculty, staff, and community members meeting frequently to discuss and participate in cultural opportunities such as enriching lectures, theater programs, and other special events. Marian's traditional dedication to teaching and caring about students continues to enhance its growing academic reputation. And the keen, campus-wide interest on the part of faculty in emerging issues in their disciplines means that dedication to the life of the mind is strong.

Athletic success: Coached by staff who care about the whole person, Marian sees athletics as an extension of the classroom. Such an approach creates success. In addition to fielding highly competitive teams in fifteen varsity sports, Marian won the National Collegiate Track Cycling Championship in 1995—defeating much larger, nationally known rivals such as Stanford University and the University of California, Berkeley.

Community outreach: Innovative on-campus and off-campus programs in service learning and mentoring now augment the classroom experience in powerful, instructive ways by involving students in reaching out and becoming mentors to their campus peers and to youngsters in nearby communities.

Also, other opportunities for volunteerism are eagerly embraced by our undergraduates. They are helping to harness the transforming power of education for human and social benefit, both in the Indianapolis area and across national borders.

Promotion of values and service: A vibrant, ecumenical campus ministry welcomes people of all faiths. It is complemented by an active collaboration between Marian and the Catholic community in Indianapolis that extends to all the dioceses of Indiana. Marian's commitment to service is further manifested in its sponsorship of the Catholic Principals Institute and partnership with local parishes in continuing education and pastoral formation programs.

Marian has traditionally done much with little. But to continue to prosper, critically important improvements in facilities and programs must be made now. The time has come for the community to support Marian College in its efforts to advance its ability to recruit, support, and educate students as effectively as possible while maintaining its distinctive mission.

Mary Rose Stockton taught chemistry at Marian College for 41 years, imparting her exceptional knowledge to future chemists, physicians and researchers. The recipient of many awards, Sr. Mary Rose has science scholarship fund at Marian named in her honor.

Dr. William Mirola, assistant professor of sociology, was selected as one of 10 sociologists nationally to participate in the "Young Scholars in American Religion" program, funded by the Pew Charitable Trusts.

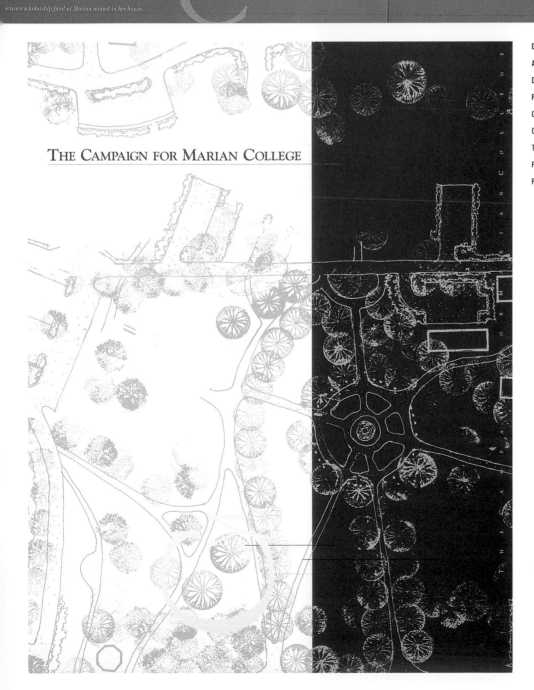

THE CAMPAIGN FOR MARIAN COLLEGE

DESIGN FIRM | Held Diedrich, Inc.
ART DIRECTOR | Dick Held
DESIGNER | Megan Snow
PHOTOGRAPHER | Larry Ladig
COPYWRITER | Marian College
CLIENT | Marian College
TOOLS | QuarkXPress
PAPER | Potlatch Vintage Velvet 80 lb. cover
PRINTING PROCESS | Offset

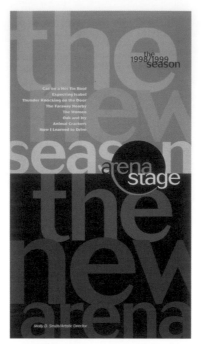

DESIGN FIRM | Mires Design
ART DIRECTORS | Scott Mires, Neill Archer Roan,
Laura Connors
DESIGNER | Miquel Perez
ILLUSTRATORS | Jody Hewgill, Mark Ulriksen
COPYWRITER | Neill Archer Roan
CLIENT | Arena Stage
TOOLS | QuarkXPress, Adobe Illustrator
PAPER | 80 lb. Cougar Opaque
PRINTING PROCESS | Web printing

It is a challenge to capture a whole season's worth of plays in one piece and convince people to sign on the dotted line. The designer's solution was to highlight each show with its own spread and personal reflections of Arena's artistic director. Since this book's publication, Arena Stage's income has exceeded previous sales figures.

Cat on a Hot Tin Roof
by Tennessee Williams
Directed by Molly D. Smith
September 11 through
October 18 in the Fichandler

We launch the 1998-99 season with a great American classic. I love this play; I am excited by the blood and the thunder and the sheer life vibrating through it. At its center is an unforgettable scene between Brick and Big Daddy. It is a scene about lies and mendacity; a theme that is always timely in Washington and which seems especially resonant today. At its heart, it tells the story of life triumphing over death, disappointment, betrayal and the past. This is my first production at Arena and Arena's first production of this play.
m.d.s.

This Pulitzer Prize-winning play has been lauded as one of the greatest American dramas of all time. With it, the celebrated author of *A Streetcar Named Desire* immortalized his vividly drawn characters of Big Daddy, Big Mamma and Maggie the Cat. In the summer heat of a Mississippi cotton plantation, Big Daddy's family gathers to celebrate his 65th birthday. Passions rise with the temperature, as painful secrets are revealed, dreams are denied, and everyone tries, like "a cat on a hot tin roof," to hold on as long as they can.

DESIGN FIRM | Lee Reedy Creative, Inc.

ART DIRECTOR | Lee Reedy

DESIGNERS | G. Patrick Gill, Heather Haworth

ILLUSTRATORS | Bob, Rob and Christian Clayton

COPYWRITER | Jamie Reedy

CLIENT | The Art Directors' Club of Denver

TOOLS | Adobe Photoshop, QuarkXPress

PRINTING PROCESS | Six-color, stochastic, embossing,
metallic inks

The design team's concept was to do a contemporary slant
on the swing era. The firm has great creative talent to
achieve the illustrations, and the copywriting captures the
swing concept perfectly.

IS Board Chairperson Barbara Finberg
and President Sara Meléndez discuss
the changing role of the independent
sector with Arianna Huffington at the
Annual Meeting.

We have a responsibility to build the strongest nonprofit and philanthropic sector possible, through leadership with vision, management with accountability, and strategic planning with research.
Sara E. Meléndez, President, INDEPENDENT SECTOR

Mission

INDEPENDENT SECTOR is
a national leadership forum,
working to encourage philan-
thropy, volunteering, not-
for-profit initiative, and citizen
action that help us better serve
people and communities.

INDEPENDENT SECTOR 1996 Annual Report

INDEPENDENT SECTOR

1996 Annual Report

DESIGN FIRM | Fernández Design
ART DIRECTOR/DESIGNER | Tracy Fernández
PHOTOGRAPHER | Stock
COPYWRITER | Elizabeth Rose
CLIENT | Independent Sector
TOOLS | QuarkXPress
PAPER | Mead Moistrite Matte, Gilbert Voice
PRINTING PROCESS | Three-color offset

This annual report was designed and produced in
ten business days on a minimal budget.

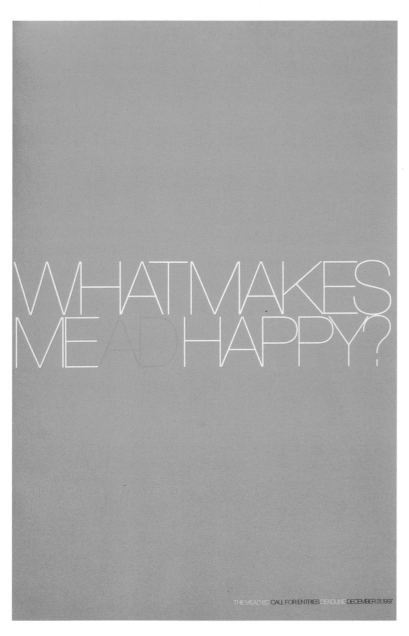

WHAT MAKES MEAD HAPPY?

THE MEAD 60 CALL FOR ENTRIES DEADLINE DECEMBER 31, 1997

DESIGN FIRM | Pinkhaus Design

ART DIRECTOR | Joel Fuller

DESIGNER | Todd Houser

PHOTOGRAPHER | Gallen Mei

COPYWRITER | Frank Cunningham

CLIENT | Mead 60: Call for Entries

TOOLS | Adobe Illustrator and Photoshop

PAPER | Signature Dull Mead 100 lb. cover

PRINTING PROCESS | Four color Process

This brochure was meant to stand out from the myriad entry forms that arrive on most designers' desks each week and to impress upon designers the prestige of winning Mead's award medal.

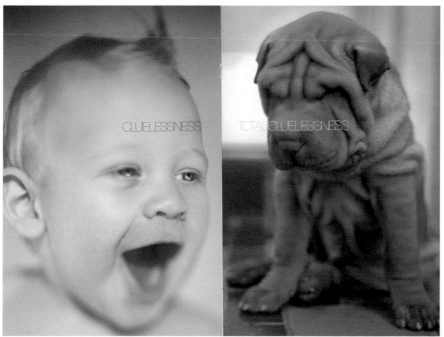

CLUELESSNESS   TOTAL CLUELESSNESS

DESIGN FIRM | Muller and Co

ALL DESIGN | Jeff Miller

ILLUSTRATORS | Jack Harris, Emory Au

PHOTOGRAPHER/COPYWRITER | Alvin Ailey

CLIENT | Alvin Ailey

TOOLS | Adobe Photoshop, QuarkXPress

PAPER | Strobe

PRINTING PROCESS | Two-color offset

The biggest thrill for Muller and Co. was receiving
their own brochures in the mail with all of the scratches,
smears, and grime that come from mailing anything.
This assignment made the design team feel as though
they were participating in the world of dance rather than
designing in a vacuum.

DESIGN FIRM | Sagmeister Inc.

ART DIRECTOR | Stefan Sagmeister

DESIGNERS | Stefan Sagmeister, Veronica Oh, Hjalti Karlsson

PHOTOGRAPHERS | Adam Fuss, Wolfgang Tillmans, et al.

COPYWRITER/CLIENT | France Morin

TOOLS | QuarkXPress, Adobe Illustrator and Photoshop

PAPER | 100 lb. matte coated

PRINTING PROCESS | Offset

This brochure for an art project featured contemporary artists working at a Shaker Community.

the quiet in the land

EVERYDAY LIFE, CONTEMPORARY ART and THE SHAKERS

Institute of Contemporary Art
@ Maine College of Art

ICA

August 9 - September 21, 1997

Opening Reception, Saturday,
August 9, 10am - 12pm

the shaker community at
sabbathday lake:
Sisters Frances A. Carr,
Marie Burgess, June Carpenter,
Minnie Greene and Brothers
Arnold Hadd, Wayne Smith, and
Alistair Bate

and artists:
Janine Antoni, Domenico de Clario,
Adam Fuss, Mona Hatoum,
Sam Samore, Jana Sterbak,
Kazumi Tanaka, Wolfgang
Tillmans, Nari Ward, and
Chen Zhen.

conceived and organized by
France Morin

exhibition at the ICA organized
with Jennifer R. Gross and the
Maine College of Art

DESIGN FIRM | Clarke Communication Design

ART DIRECTOR/DESIGNER | John V. Clarke

PHOTOGRAPHERS | John V. Clarke, students

COPYWRITER | William Harris

CLIENT | University of Illinois at Urbana—Champaign
for the School of Art and Design

TOOLS | QuarkXPress, Adobe Photoshop

PRINTING PROCESS | Offset lithography

Entitled Positions Available, this was the first catalog
done for an exhibition of graduate students' artwork.
The budget was limited, so all photography was provided
by the artists themselves. John Clarke shot additional
black-and-white photos at a local exhibition of the
students' work, to add visual impact to the catalog.

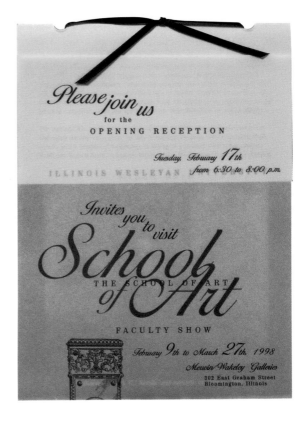

DESIGN FIRM | Illinois Wesleyan University

ART DIRECTOR/DESIGNER | Sherilyn McElroy

PHOTOGRAPHER | Kevin Strandberg

CLIENT | Merwin School of Art, Wakeley Galleries

TOOLS | QuarkXPress

PRINTING PROCESS | Offset

The design goal was to create a brochure that could be used both as a gallery announcement and as a recruiting enticement for prospective students (the top vellum page can be removed for recruiting). McElroy's intent in the design was to unify disparate artistic techniques: differing styles, media, and sizes.

DESIGN FIRM | Bentley College, Communication and Publications

ART DIRECTOR | Amy Coates

COPYWRITER | Jennifer Spira

CLIENT | Bentley College, Student Activities

TOOLS | QuarkXPress, Adobe Photoshop

PAPER | Zanders Mega Gloss 80 lb. text

PRINTING PROCESS | Digital

To meet the client's deadline without sacrificing quality, the designer used digital printing, an inexpensive print method that delivers a four-color finished product in as little as four days.

les·week-ends culturels

février
mars 1998

cinéma danse musique documentaires émotions

Télé-Québec

DESIGN FIRM | Sonia Poirier
ART DIRECTOR/DESIGNER | Sonia Poirier
PHOTOGRAPHER | Georges Dufaux
COPYWRITER | Suzie Koberge
CLIENT | Tele-Quebec
TOOLS | QuarkXPress, Adobe Photoshop
PAPER | Rolland Supreme Dull
PRINTING PROCESS | Two-color offset

This brochure promotes the two-month series of artistic
programs translated as cultural weekends.

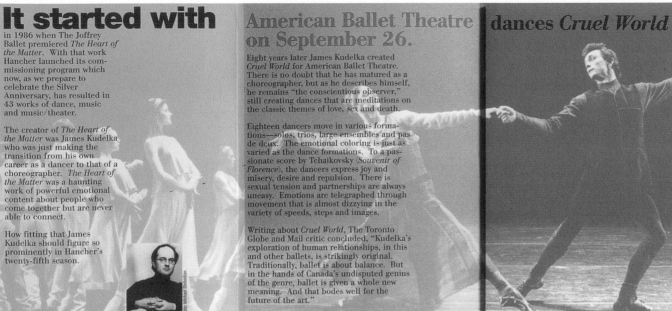

It started with

in 1986 when The Joffrey Ballet premiered *The Heart of the Matter*. With that work Hancher launched its commissioning program which now, as we prepare to celebrate the Silver Anniversary, has resulted in 43 works of dance, music and music/theater.

The creator of *The Heart of the Matter* was James Kudelka who was just making the transition from his own career as a dancer to that of a choreographer. *The Heart of the Matter* was a haunting work of powerful emotional content about people who come together but are never able to connect.

How fitting that James Kudelka should figure so prominently in Hancher's twenty-fifth season.

American Ballet Theatre dances *Cruel World* on September 26.

Eight years later James Kudelka created *Cruel World* for American Ballet Theatre. There is no doubt that he has matured as a choreographer, but as he describes himself, he remains "the conscientious observer," still creating dances that are meditations on the classic themes of love, sex and death.

Eighteen dancers move in various formations—solos, trios, large ensembles and pas de deux. The emotional coloring is just as varied as the dance formations. To a passionate score by Tchaikovsky (*Souvenir of Florence*), the dancers express joy and misery, desire and repulsion. There is sexual tension and partnerships are always uneasy. Emotions are telegraphed through movement that is almost dizzying in the variety of speeds, steps and images.

Writing about *Cruel World*, The Toronto Globe and Mail critic concluded, "Kudelka's exploration of human relationships, in this and other ballets, is strikingly original. Traditionally, ballet is about balance. But in the hands of Canada's undisputed genius of the genre, ballet is given a whole new meaning. And that bodes well for the future of the art."

ART DIRECTOR/DESIGNER | Ron McClellen
COPYWRITER | Judith Hurtig
CLIENT | Hancher Auditorium
TOOLS | Adobe PageMaker and Photoshop, Macintosh
PAPER | Stock Simpson Sundance Felt
PRINTING PROCESS | Offset

This small-budget brochure was sent to dance patrons and ticket buyers to inform them on the connections between the choreographer, the director, the company, and past presentations of dance at Hanch

DESIGN FIRM | River City Studio
ALL DESIGN | Jennifer Elliott
COPYWRITER | Dennis Pruitt
CLIENT | Rick's Place
TOOLS | QuarkXPress, Adobe Illustrator and Photoshop
PAPER | Starbrite, Opaque 80 lb. cover
PRINTING PROCESS | Five PMS lithography

Rick's Place invitation booklet presented a two-fold problem: how to educate recipients about the foundation and convince them to attend a fundraiser. The designer's single solution was to make this invitation as exciting as the feel-good party of the summer!

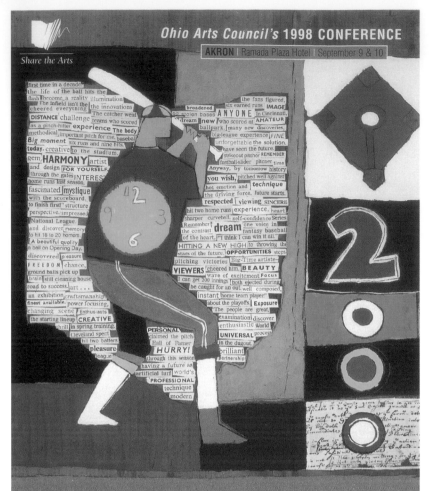

DESIGN FIRM | Base Art Company

ART DIRECTOR/DESIGNER | Terry Alan Rohrbach

ILLUSTRATOR | Kirk Richard Smith

COPYWRITER | Charles Fenton, Editor

CLIENT | Ohio Arts Council

TOOLS | QuarkXPress, Adobe Photoshop,
Macromedia FreeHand

PAPER | Mohawk Navajo

PRINTING PROCESS | Four-color process plus two PMS

Themed Batting 2000: Facing the Fastball of Change, the brochure/return registration form draws inspiration from the obvious. Textural qualities of the cover illustration were retained throughout the piece in headers and backgrounds. Event speakers were displayed in line-ups according to their day of appearance.

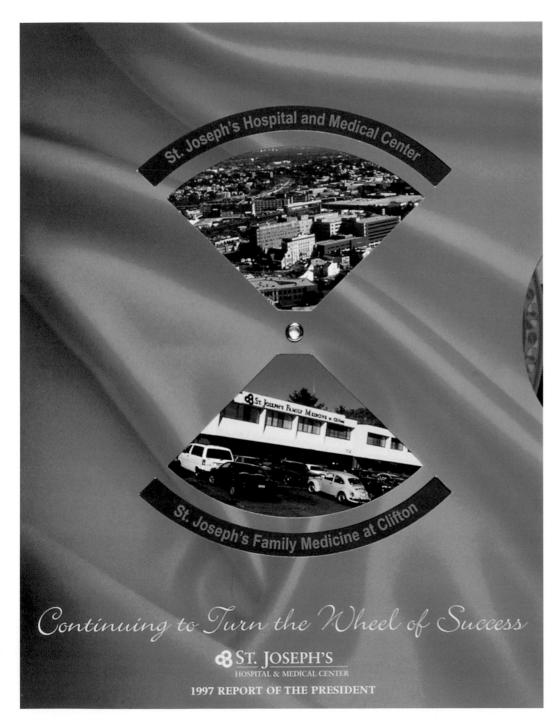

DESIGN FIRM | St. Joseph's Hospital
ALL DESIGN | Ken Morris, Jr.
PHOTOGRAPHER | Rich Green
COPYWRITER | Sister Jane Frances
CLIENT | St. Joseph's Hospital and Medical Center
TOOLS | QuarkXPress, Adobe Illustrator and Photoshop
PAPER | Warren Lustro Dull
PRINTING PROCESS | Six-color process, spot and varnish

The cover design was inspired by the proportional scale artists use to resize artwork. The designer used this element to encourage viewers to interact with the design. Due to budget restraints, he was limited to four colors on the cover, but by enlarging the black-and-white photos to full pages and surrounding them with decorative color borders, he was able to add color to the inside pages.

DESIGN FIRM | Gackle Anderson Henningsen, Inc.
DESIGNER/ILLUSTRATOR | Wendy Anderson
PHOTOGRAPHER | Mike Newell
COPYWRITER | Greg Gackle
CLIENT | Bettendorf Public Library
TOOLS | QuarkXPress, Adobe Photoshop, Power Center Pro
PAPER | Consolidated Productolith
PRINTING PROCESS | Four-color process

This brochure was designed to be bold and eye-catching, like the newly renovated library it describes. Sculpted faces accent the services provided, from the forefront of technology to the intimate café.

DESIGN FIRM | Hoffman & Angelic Design

ART DIRECTOR/DESIGNER | Andrea Hoffman

ILLUSTRATOR | Ivan Angelic

HAND LETTERERS | Ivan Angelic, Michael and Suzanne Cohen

CLIENT | Seattle Study Club

TOOLS | Adobe Illustrator

PAPER | Neenah Environment, UV Ultra II, Simpson Quest

PRINTING PROCESS | Offset and foil

The design team created an elegant manner with an approachable feel in this brochure by using bold zen-like brush illustrations, hand-lettered quotations, and the juxtaposition of textures against matte uncoated stock. Speckled UV fly sheets revealed bold illustrations beneath. The natural, serene color scheme of sand, sage, and terra-cotta, and the square and circle elements, balanced harmoniously and elegantly.

The Three Arts Club of Chicago presents our eighth annual Landmark Jazz Series: **ecLecTica**

It is with great pride that we open this season with pianist Jodie Christian. A life-long South-sider, Christian has kept the best of company, recording with jazz greats Stan Getz, Lester Young, Coleman Hawkins, and Chet Baker, to name just a few. Downbeat Magazine says, "Christian offers the straight ahead, purely musical side of bop... lyricism with a crystal touch is the heart and soul of his art."

joDie cHrisTian
September 23, 1998

karL montzKa quarTet
November 18, 1998

Karl Montzka brings his Hammond organ and his innovative quartet for an evening of smooth and swinging jazz. Montzka is emerging on the local scene as **a gifted band leader, organist, arranger and composer, exploring everything from street beat grooves to bright swing.** Joining Montzka in the quartet are his brother Eric on drums, guitarist John McLean and Ryan Schultz on bass trumpet.

paTriciA barBer
January 27, 1999

Patricia Barber is noted for her gorgeous voice, depth of vision and fresh, incisive interpretations. A leader on the local scene for the past decade, Ms. Barber was named the #1 "Female Jazz Vocal Talent Deserving Wider Recognition" by Downbeat's International Critics poll. Thomas Conrad of Stereophile magazine wrote of her work, "**If you've lived it yourself, you can sing to people ...and they will not only love it, they will need it.**"

This acoustic jazz quartet delivers what Lloyd Sachs of the Chicago SunTimes calls "**...hard-bopping delights and flowing meditations by a band that deserves to go places.**" Leaders Brian Gephart (saxophone) and Bob Long (piano) are joined by Ken Haebich on bass and Mark Otto on drums. All of these artists have outstanding reputations for their work, both locally and nationally, and together they deliver an evening of extraordinary jazz.

briAn gePhart bOb long quarTet
March 24, 1999

Recipient of the 1998 Back Stage Bistro award for outstanding achievement, Audrey Morris graces Landmark Jazz ® with her outstanding vocal and piano talents. The former resident pianist/vocalist for Mr. Kelly's and a member of the in-house trio at the legendary London House, Ms. Morris has played with such luminaries as Oscar Peterson, Carmen McRae and Bobby Short. Howard Reich, writing for the Chicago Tribune said, "**A local treasure by any standard, Morris reaffirms her place at the pinnacle of seasoned singer-pianists with utterly unaffected, haunting readings of standards.**"

audRey morRis
May 26, 1999

DESIGN FIRM | WATCH! Graphic Design
DESIGNER | Carolyn Chester
CLIENT | The Three Arts Club of Chicago
TOOLS | Adobe Illustrator, QuarkXPress
PAPER | Cougar
PRINTING PROCESS | Two PMS plus black

Landmark Jazz is a bimonthly series featuring live performances by Chicago's most distinguished jazz artists. The design is inspired by early jazz albums.

On the brochure cover:

WISCONSIN
FOUNDATION
for
SCHOOL MUSIC

"WITH MUSIC, GREATNESS SEEMS LIKE IT'S
RIGHT AROUND THE CORNER."

Amanda Evers,

Freedom Middle School

On the pledge form:

WFSM DONOR PLEDGE FORM

ANNUAL DONATION

...invest in education for a solid future. Please become our partner in providing ...students with valuable life experiences through music. Annual donors will be ...recognized in the following ways.

...- $199
Recognition in State Honors Concert Programs and other printed material

...- $999
Above recognition plus engraved Wisconsin Foundation for School Music Key Tag

...and above   Above recognition plus engraved Wisconsin Foundation for School Music Key Tag and the latest CD releases of the nine Wisconsin State Honors performing groups

...an annual donation of $_____ to the Wisconsin ...on for School Music.

...PMENT FUND

...awards which recognize student achievement by donating $_____

...a student in the State Honors Music Project by donating $_____.

...formances the best they can be by donating $_____ to provide ...r student use.

...UND

...consin Foundation for School Music's Endowment Fund ...t projects and scholarships of the Wisconsin School ..._____ to the Foundation's Endowment Fund.

...ORIALS

...ntury by establishing a memorial, creating a ...nth options. Special recognition will be given ...who support these funds. Please contact us ...s, or other ways to honor special individuals.

...is enclosed in full. ...xceeds $200. Please bill me:
...ll Amount   ☐ Semi-Annually   ☐ Quarterly

...   State: _____   Zip: _____

WISCONSIN
FOUNDATION for
SCHOOL MUSIC

THANK YOU FOR YOUR GENEROUS COMMITMENT TO WISCONSIN YOUTH!

Checks should be made out and mailed to:
Wisconsin Foundation for School Music
4797 Hayes Road, Madison, WI 53704
608-249-4366 • lpeterson@wsmaf.com

DESIGN FIRM | 1049 Design
ART DIRECTOR | Rachel Lom, Wisconsin Foundation for
School Music (WFSM)
DESIGNERS/ILLUSTRATORS | Mary Kay Warner, 1049 Design
PHOTOGRAPHERS | Rick Trummer, Don Christensen
COPYWRITERS | Rachel Lom, Linda Peterson, WFSM
CLIENT | Wisconsin Foundation for School Music
TOOLS | QuarkXPress, Adobe Illustrator
PAPER | 80 lb. Productolith Gloss cover; 100 lb.
Productolith Gloss text

To achieve a creative, rich design on a two-color
budget, textures, duotones, and many different
screens were used. Photos and quotes from kids
provided a personal connection to their music.

DESIGN FIRM | Sayles Graphic Design

ALL DESIGN | John Sayles

COPYWRITER | Kristin Lennert

CLIENT | National Society of Fund Raising Executives

PAPER | Astro Brite Goldenrod

PRINTING PROCESS | Offset

Professional fundraisers group wanted an attention-getting campaign package for its 1998 regional gathering. When the initial design (themed: Raising Dough: Recipes for Success) was presented at the 1997 annual meeting, each attendee received a bakery bread bag printed with the theme and filled with a fresh loaf of bread. The later mailing included a wooden spoon tied inside the box and an informational brochure.

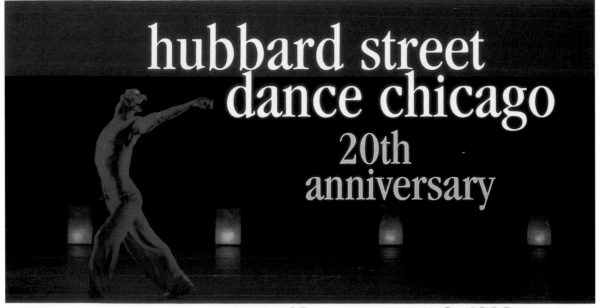

hubbard street
dance chicago
20th
anniversary

APRIL 14 THROUGH MAY 3, 1998
auditorium theatre

DESIGN FIRM | Fernández Design

ART DIRECTOR/DESIGNER | Tracy Fernández

PHOTOGRAPHERS | Lois Greenfield, Gert Krautbauer

COPYWRITER | Michael Pauren

CLIENT | Hubbard Street Dance Chicago

TOOLS | QuarkXPress

PAPER | Utopia I

PRINTING PROCESS | Four-color offset

This brochure was designed and produced within
one week. The design goal was to create an interesting
direct-mail piece that is easy to follow

DESIGN FIRM | Solar Design
ART DIRECTOR | Jennifer Schmidt
DESIGNERS | Jennifer Schmidt, Susan Russellu
COPYWRITER | Bill Watson
CLIENT | Maryville City of Youth
TOOLS | QuarkXPress, Adobe Photoshop
PAPER | Neenah Classic Crest 80 lb. cover
PRINTING PROCESS | Four-color offset

This brochure promotes the Chicagoland Sports
Hall of Fame facility.

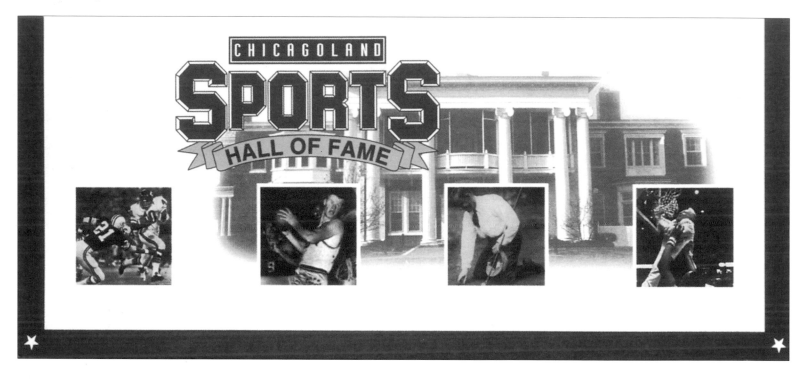

DESIGN FIRM | Fernández Design
ART DIRECTOR/DESIGNER | Tracy Fernández
PHOTOGRAPHERS | Lois Greenfield, Reudi Hoffman
COPYWRITER | Michael Pauken
CLIENT | Hubbard Street Dance Chicago
TOOLS | QuarkXPress
PAPER | Mead Signature Gloss 100 lb. text and cover
PRINTING PROCESS | Four-color plus one PMS plus
aqueous coat

The objective was to have an attractive piece that
would celebrate the 20th anniversary season of the
company and that could also be sold as a souvenir at
performances. Photos were taken with a telephoto
lens at performances. The production time was two
weeks, and the budget was minimal.

Twentieth Anniversary Album

HUBBARD STREET DANCE CHICAGO

"On their 20th Anniversary... Hubbard Street Dance Chicago is soaring." Richard Christiansen, Chicago Tribune

Hubbard Street Dance Chicago
Celebrates 20 Years

DESIGN FIRM | GAF Advertising/Design

ALL DESIGN | Gregg A. Floyd

PHOTOGRAPHER | David Obar

COPYWRITERS | Gregg A. Floyd, Linda Bryza

CLIENT | Ft. Worth Housing Authority: Amaka
Childcare Center

TOOLS | QuarkXPress, Adobe Illustrator and Photoshop

PAPER | Confetti, cover; Productolith, text

PRINTING PROCESS | 1/1 spot, cover; 4/4 process, text

A revitalization program was created to build a day-care center in a low-income development. The logo concept and brochure had to reflect the name of the center and the theme of investing in the future.

WILIJAH WILL BE WANTED, TOO.

MOST OF THE KIDS THAT GREW UP IN WILIJAH'S NEIGHBORHOOD ARE NOW WANTED

DESIGN FIRM | GAF Advertising/Design

ART DIRECTOR/DESIGNER | Gregg A. Floyd

PHOTOGRAPHER | Ken Brock

COPYWRITER | Gregg A. Floyd

CLIENT | St. Philip's School and Community Center

TOOLS | QuarkXPress, Adobe Illustrator and Photoshop

PAPER | Genesis

PRINTING PROCESS | 2/2 spot color

This brochure was created to generate underwriting for low-income students' tuition. The design succeeded by increasing awareness and participation in the program.

DESIGN FIRM | GAF Advertising/Design

ART DIRECTOR/DESIGNER | Gregg A. Floyd

ILLUSTRATORS | *The Wall Street Journal* Art Department,
Gregg A. Floyd

PHOTOGRAPHERS | Jess Hornbuckle, David Obar,
Linda Bryza, Alice Sykes, Kelly Buizch

COPYWRITER | Gregg A. Floyd

CLIENT | Dallas Housing Authority

TOOLS | QXD, Adobe Illustrator and Photoshop

PAPER | Environmental

PRINTING PROCESS | 1/1 spot color

This biennial report's theme reflects the mission of using education and DHA programs as the equation to move low-income people towards self-sufficiency. The design incorporates a community newspaper style to describe program and individual successes.

DESIGN FIRM | Sayles Graphic Design
ALL DESIGN | John Sayles
COPYWRITER | Jack Carey
CLIENT | Des Moines Parks and Recreation Department
PAPER | Crown Vintage Antique White
PRINTING PROCESS | Offset

A series of activities meant a versatile invitation was needed, since not all guests would attend each event. Sayles' solution was an elegant collection of cards, each printed with the time and location for individual events. Copper and black ink are used on cream paper; the hand-tied ribbon references the ribbon cutting and adds an unexpected touch. The trimmed cards fit into a black #10 envelope that can be mailed with one postage stamp. To commemorate the event, each invitation included an oversized Lucite lapel pin printed in metallic copper and silver inks.

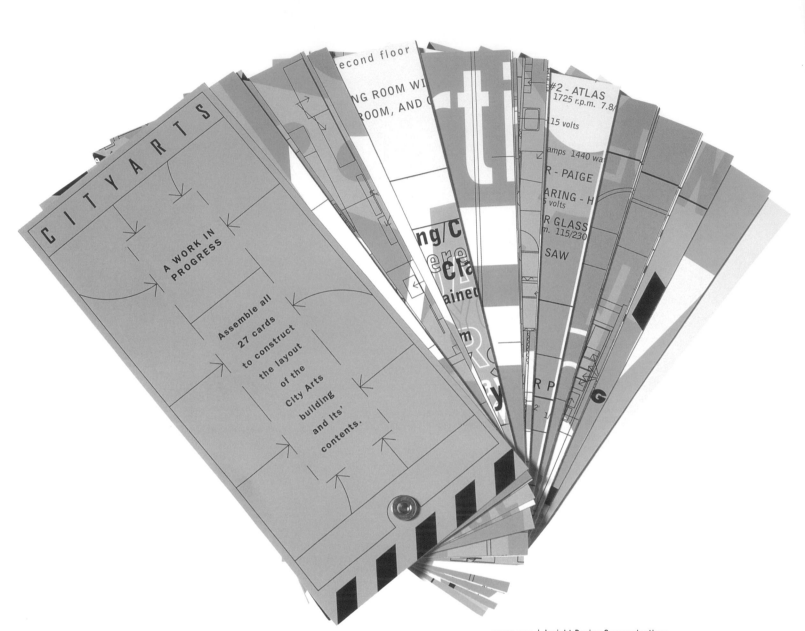

DESIGN FIRM | Insight Design Communications
ART DIRECTORS | Tracy and Sherrie Holdeman
DESIGNERS | Sherrie Holdeman, Chris Parks
ILLUSTRATOR | Chris Parks
PHOTOGRAPHER | Dimitris Skliris
CLIENT | City Arts
TOOLS | Macromedia FreeHand

Since this art event took place in a partially finished gallery, where actual construction was taking place, the brochure took on a functional construction theme. Aside from developing construction icons, the pages assemble into a functional blueprint layout of the building and gallery itself.

it's a boy!

Last year nearly 1,500 newborns began life in a place where the guiding rule is compassionate, comprehensive care.

The Maternal/Child Unit at Lake Cumberland Regional Hospital allows parents to labor, deliver and recover in a loving family environment. Brothers, sisters and grandparents are encouraged to share in feeding and holding the newest family member in a warm, homelike setting with maximum support and minimum stress.

And when some newborns require intensive care, our Special Care Nursery is certified to handle all but the most critically ill babies.

Do you know who we are?

A Report to the Community

DESIGN FIRM | Kirby Stephens Design

ART DIRECTOR/DESIGNER | Kirby Stephens

PHOTOGRAPHER | William Cox, stock

COPYWRITER | Kirby Stephens

CLIENT | Lake Cumberland Regional Hospital

TOOLS | Macromedia FreeHand, Adobe Photoshop

PAPER | Repap Matte

PRINTING PROCESS | Five-color spot, offset

To help mend a local hospital's waning reputation, new management gave the designers specific areas to address in this direct, to-the-point, report to the community.

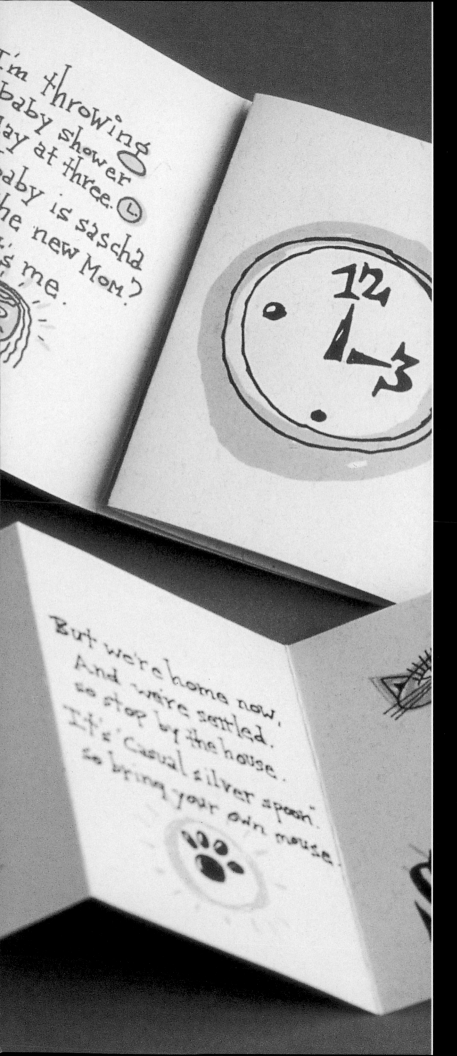

PROMOTIONAL
BROCHURES

DESIGN FIRM | Sayles Graphic Design
ALL DESIGN | John Sayles
COPYWRITER | Annie Meacham
PAPER | Terracoat Gray
PRINTING PROCESS | Offset

This one-color invitation uses storytelling graphics: a shower on the front and an airplane hopping from one home to the next. The piece folds out to reveal the recipient of the baby shower—an adopted kitten named Sascha B.

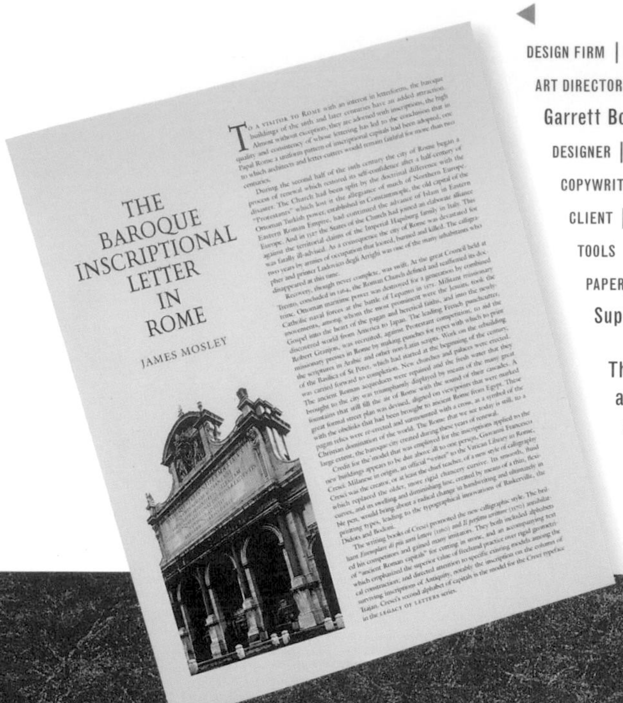

DESIGN FIRM | Letter Design

ART DIRECTORS | Paul Shaw,
Garrett Boge

DESIGNER | Paul Shaw

COPYWRITER | James Mosley

CLIENT | Letter Perfect

TOOLS | Macintosh IIci

PAPER/PRINTING | Mohawk
Superfine, Studley Press

This essay was commissioned
and designed to promote three
new historically-inspired type-
faces. The look of the essay
is meant to reflect the late
Renaissance while remaining
contemporary.

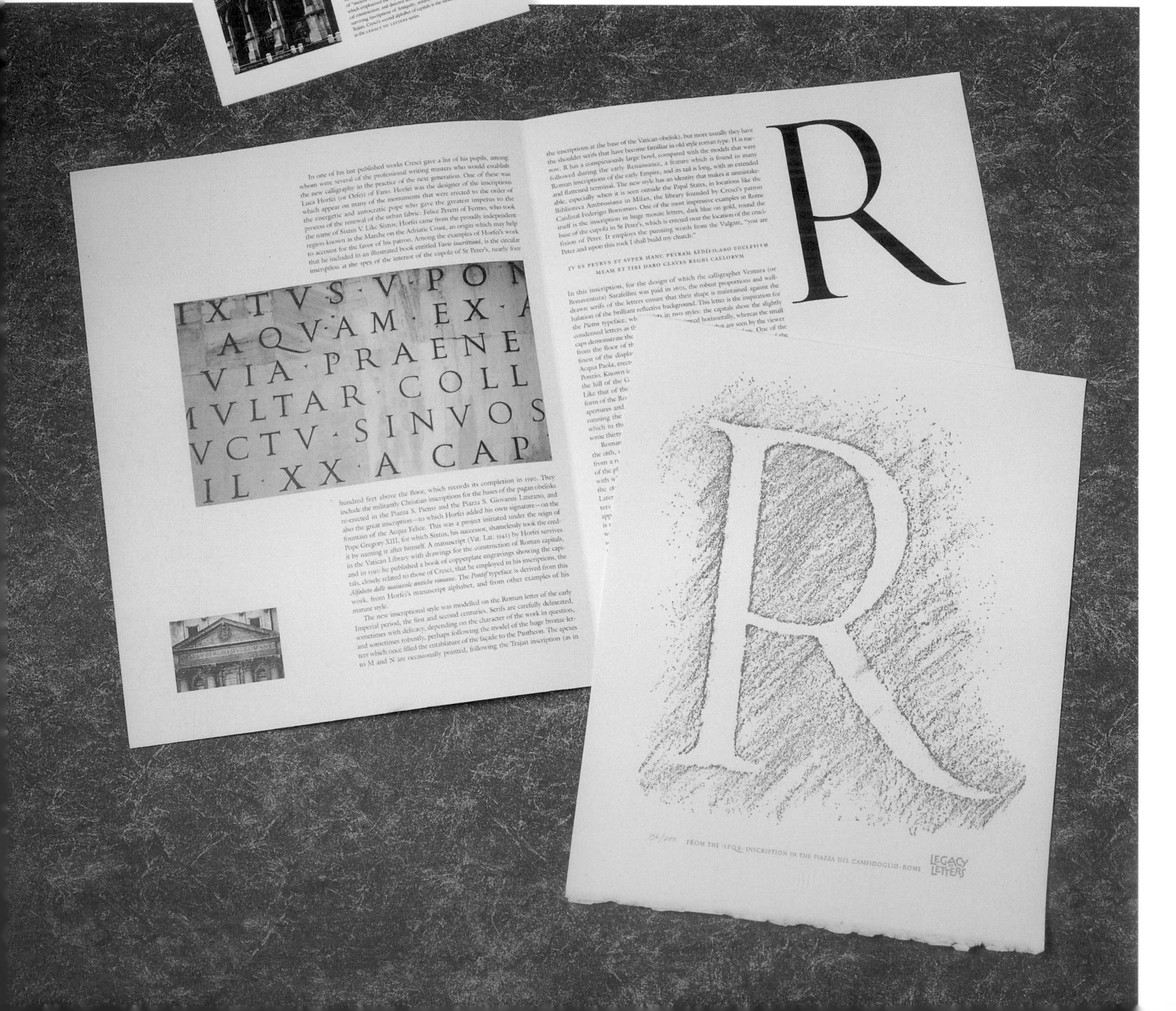

THE
BAROQUE
INSCRIPTIONAL
LETTER
IN
ROME

JAMES MOSLEY

DESIGN FIRM | Metalli Lindberg
Advertising
CREATIVE DIRECTOR | Lionello Borean
ART DIRECTOR | Stefano Dal Tin
COPYWRITER | Corrado Casteuri
CLIENT | Cappamobili SRL
TOOLS | Adobe Illustrator,
Adobe Photoshop

The piece concentrates on presenting
the unique products offered by the
client. From the function and meaning
of the door for furniture, to its normal
movement, concepts that outline the
advantages of a relationship with Cap-
pamobili are used throughout the
brochure.

Open and Closed.

Let's Get This Show

Pop Wagner and

Stoney Lonesome

On The Road!

DESIGN FIRM | MartinRoss Design

DESIGNERS | Martin Skoro, Ross Rezac

COPYWRITER | Patricia McKernon

CLIENT | Pop Wagner and Stoney Lonesome

TOOLS | QuarkXPress

PAPER/PRINTING | Coated paper/
Four-color process

Using existing photos, the client wanted a
brochure that would stand out from other
promotions. A die-cut was used to make
the distinction, and color, playful use of
type, and trimmed photos were used
to appeal to the people who booked
shows.

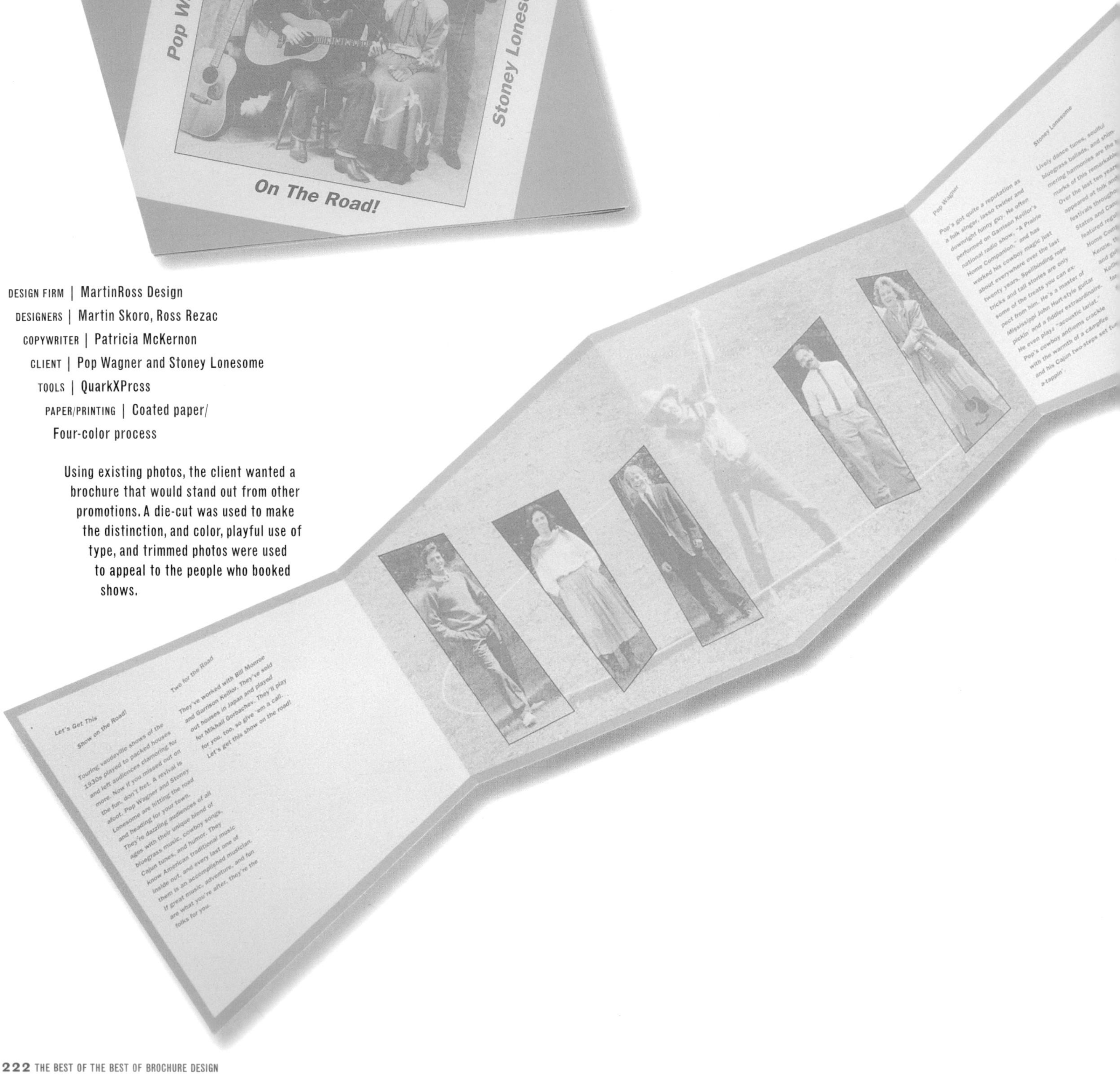

DESIGN FIRM | Metalli Lindberg
Advertising
CREATIVE DIRECTOR | Lionello Borean
ART DIRECTOR | Stefano Dal Tin
TOOLS | Adobe Illustrator,
Adobe Photoshop
PAPER | Fedrigoni Freelife

Ecosphera, a new way of distributing
organic food products, is featured in this
retailer-focused brochure that includes
a non-profit philosophy that pays attention to the market. Mailed in a brown
paper bag that is usually used for bread,
the nature of ecosphera is suggested,
and the piece acts as a pun about food
and consuming information.

The brochure cards show the following text:

campus visit
hotels   museum
...grants
crafts cluster   enameling   metals
...amics   fiber
student... sports teams   clubs
stude...
portfolio preparation
design   ...position   craft
design cluster   graphic design   industrial design
...design   medical illustration
ill...
faculty   encourage   create   nurture
...vide
transfer students   credits   portfolios
reviews   transcripts   ...
financial aid   grants   work study
...scholarships   loans
awards
career services   college teaching
art administration   freelance

fine arts
at the Cleveland Institute of Art

Educating the total artist is a concept you'll hear quite a lot about at the Cleveland Institute of Art. Since 1882, we've been dedicated to graduating artists and designers who are also thinkers and innovators: creative problem solvers with exceptional skills and a strong background in the basics, as well as a wide exposure to many disciplines.

DESIGN FIRM | Nesnadny and Schwartz
ART DIRECTOR | Michelle Moehler
DESIGNERS | Michelle Moehler, Melissa Petrollini
ILLUSTRATOR | Melissa Petrollini
COPYWRITER | Cleveland Institute of Art
CLIENT | Cleveland Institute of Art
TOOLS | QuarkXPress, Macromedia FreeHand, Adobe Photoshop, Adobe Illustrator
PAPER/PRINTING | Warren Lustro 80 lb. dull, Fortran printing

This new series of brochures was created as a recruiting tool for the Cleveland Institute of Art. Intended for prospective students, they are mailed in a sequence designed for each recipient to communicate details about the college and its programs.

DESIGN FIRM | Emerson, Wajdowicz Studios
ART DIRECTOR | Jurek Wajdowicz
DESIGNERS | Lisa LaRochelle,
Jurek Wajdowicz
COPYWRITERS | Eugene Richards,
Daiv Konigsberg
CLIENT | Island Paper Mills,
Division of E. B. Eddy Forest Products, Ltd.
PAPER/PRINTING | Bravo/Offset

This brochure is the first in the Bravo Photo Masters series, presenting a sampling of the best photo journalism in the world. It was created to intertwine and appropriately merge photography, design, and typography into one expressive and unique form.

BRAVORICHARDS

Blind Elder, Guinea: "I am unnerved because he can't see me. Then he touches my face, and a connection is made." Eugene Richards/USA, Bravo Photo Masters Series, Issue 1 from Island Paper Mills.

DESIGN FIRM | Greteman Group

DESIGNERS | Sonia Greteman, James Strange

ILLUSTRATOR | James Strange

COPYWRITER | Allison Sedlacek

CLIENT | Wichita Industries and Services for the Blind

TOOLS | Macromedia FreeHand

PAPER/PRINTING | Cougar White/Offset printing

This annual report transcends service as a vehicle for financial accountability by focusing on what it means to be blind. Bold graphics and actual quotes walk readers through the isolation, risk taking, and challenges faced by people with low vision. Die cuts illustrate their different perspective, while embossing conveys their greater reliance on touch.

Taking **risks** requires courage and encouragement.

"It's easier because I have family, but it's also hard emotionally sometimes to do things on your own. I want to know I can do it."

See

See the world in a different way.

WICHITA INDUSTRIES AND SERVICES FOR THE BLIND, INC.

1995 ANNUAL REPORT

...IF SOMEONE WILL KEEP ASKING HIM THESE SAME QUESTIONS OFTEN AND IN VARIOUS FORMS, YOU CAN BE SURE THAT IN THE END HE WILL KNOW ABOUT THEM AS ACCURATELY AS ANYBODY.

THE GREATEST REWARD WILL
BE A PERSONAL CHANGE
THAT EXPANDS YOU IN A WAY
THAT YOU MIGHT NEVER HAVE
DREAMED OF...IT OPENED UP
A WHOLE NEW RANGE OF
POSSIBILITIES THAT I WOULD
NEVER HAVE COME TO WITHOUT
THE COACHING PROCESS OF
NEW VENTURES WEST."

"WHAT IS DIFFERENT ABOUT
FLAHERTY'S APPROACH IS
THAT IT IS ABOUT SUSTAINING
CHANGES, BOTH INDIVIDUALLY
AND ORGANIZATIONALLY.
PRAGMATIC, RIGOROUS AND
COMPASSIONATE, FLAHERTY
WORKS WITHIN THE UNIQUENESS
THAT EACH PERSON REPRESENTS,
UNLEASHING THEIR PERSONAL
EFFECTIVENESS IN AMAZING,
BREAKTHROUGH WAYS."

—Sarita Chawla
Editor, Learning
Organizations

—Ken Murphy
Co-founder,
Metalens Consulting
Former Comptroller,
Pacific Bell

COACHING: A Competence for All Times—Especially Now

Coaching has always existed in human communities. Whenever someone wished to pass along accumulated wisdom or practical know-how in a way that left the recipient competent and engaged in learning, coaching was present. This is as true today as it was in Plato's time. That's why coaching is a core competence for those engaged in developing learning organizations. In fact, in our world now, coaching can provide an essential powerful methodology for developing people so that they are both more competent and more fulfilled.

Our contemporary world is full of rapid change in which no one can predict which technologies, institutions or organizations will flourish, which will fade. Certainty is scarce. There is little time for theoretical discussions, yet people must quickly make choices, allocate resources, rapidly adapt and stay highly competent. Simultaneously these same people need a sense of purpose, of meaning—that what they're doing matters and fits with what's most important to them. It seems a daunting task to build competence and encourage fulfillment within this environment. Yet that's what coaches do. They're rigorous in their standards, yet flexible enough to suit individual people and unique circumstances.

Coaches build competence, foster personal fulfillment and open up possibilities by drawing upon the knowledge of what's unchanging about human life and taking into account that which is particular about our times. To be useful, of course, coaching must be eminently practical and be helpful in both the immediate and the long term. Coaching can only accomplish all this when it's practiced by people who are highly skilled, experienced, and models of what they represent. Our program, *The Professional Coaching Course*, produces such people.

NEW VENTURES WEST
PROFESSIONAL
COACHING COURSE

DESIGN FIRM | Clark Design
ART DIRECTOR | Annemarie Clark
DESIGNER | Dan Doherty
COPYWRITER | Stacy Flaherty
CLIENT | New Ventures West
TOOLS | QuarkXPress, Adobe Photoshop
PAPER/PRINTING | Cover, Sundance 65 lb.
maize, text, Karma 100 lb. natural

The brochure needed to be designed to accompany existing collateral materials. The client wanted the piece to visually represent the fact that the company's techniques are grounded in historical teaching. Present-day mentor/student images were used in combination with those of the past, along with the use of the Greek column to represent history, a strong foundation, and education.

CYRIX 1996 ANNUAL REPORT

DESIGN FIRM | Sullivan Perkins
ALL DESIGN | Kelly Allen
COPYWRITER | Elizabeth Gluckman
CLIENT | Cyrix
PAPER/PRINTING | Fortune/WORX

Cyrix, a computer chip company, wanted to show new products and advancements. The message was carried through the piece by choosing appropriate highway signage and background.

DESIGN FIRM | Aerial

ART DIRECTOR/DESIGNER | Tracy Moon

CLIENT | Hotel Boheme/San Francisco

TOOLS | Adobe Photoshop, Live Picture, QuarkXPress

This brochure is for a small, North Beach San Francisco hotel with a fifties, Bohemian style and decor. All pattern, imagery, and photography in the piece draw directly from the hotel itself and the Beat-era time period.

DESIGN FIRM | Melissa Passehl Design
ART DIRECTOR/DESIGNER | Melissa Passehl
ILLUSTRATOR | Melissa Passehl
CLIENT | Berryessa Union School District

The objective of the "Success for All Learners in School and in Life" brochure was to present an overview of a new curriculum to teachers who instruct grades 1–8. The illustrations and bright colors remind the reviewer of the ultimate audience who benefits from the program.

SUCCESS FOR ALL LEARNERS IN SCHOOL & IN LIFE

SCORING RUBRIC-ARCHEOLOGICAL LOG

4 Six areas for the log are addressed. There are few, if any grammatical errors. It includes colored detailed illustrations and explanations. It is historically accurate. The presentation is neat and creative. and all members have shared the work equally.

3 All areas are addressed. It is historically accurate. It includes color illustrations and complete explanations. There are few grammatical errors. The presentation is neat, and all members have shared the work equally.

2 At least five areas are addressed. It includes color illustrations and fair explanations. There are some grammatical errors. The presentation is neat, and all members have shared the work equally.

1 At least four areas are addressed. It contains many historical errors. It includes color illustrations and limited explanations. There are grammatical errors. The presentation is poor.

SCORING RUBRIC-COMPARISON CHART

4 Your chart is historically accurate and your life experiences are detailed and complete. It includes colored, detailed illustrations and explanations. There are few, if any, grammatical errors. The presentation is neat and creative. All members participated.

3 Your chart is historically accurate and your life experiences are complete. It includes color illustrations and complete explanations. There are few grammatical errors.

2 Your chart contains some historical errors. There are some grammatical errors. Your life experiences and your life experiences are shown. The presentation is neat. It includes color illustrations and fair explanations.

1 Your chart may contain historical errors. Your life experiences are unclear. It includes illustrations and limited explanations. There are grammatical errors. The presentation is poor.

CONCLUSION:

THE USE OF A SPECIFIC GRAPHIC ORGANIZER IS ONLY ONE WAY A TEACHER CAN ALIGN STANDARDS, INSTRUCTION AND METHODS OF ASSESSMENT TO HELP STUDENTS SUCCESSFULLY MEET OR EXCEED THE IDENTIFIED STANDARDS. ANY FORMAT CAN BE USED AS LONG AS IT INCLUDES THE ESSENTIAL INTEGRATED INGREDIENTS:

1. The content and life-long learning standards that will be taught.
2. A method of assessing students' application of skills and knowledge;
3. The complex reasoning process embedded in the performance task;
4. The instructional strategies for the content standard(s) and the complex reasoning process(es); and
5. The instructional materials.

PERFORMANCE-BASED GRADUATION

PERFORMANCE-BASED GRADUATION REFLECTS WHAT THE REAL WORLD REQUIRES. IN A JOB SETTING, A WORK-ER IS NOT REWARDED FOR SIMPLY BEING THERE, BUT IS ASSESSED ON THE QUALITY OF HIS OR HER PERFORMANCE. SIMILARLY, THE GRADUATION DIPLOMA WILL NOT BE BASED ON TIME SPENT IN CLASS. RATHER, STUDENTS WILL QUALIFY FOR GRADUATION BY DEMONSTRATING THEIR KNOWLEDGE AND SKILLS IN THE TRADITIONAL SUBJECT AREAS — CONTENT STANDARDS — AND BY DEMONSTRATING THEIR KNOWLEDGE AND SKILLS IN OF WORK PLACE COMPETENCIES — LIFELONG LEARNING STANDARDS. STUDENTS WILL NOT ONLY DEMON-STRATE ACHIEVEMENT OF THESE KNOWLEDGE AND SKILLS THROUGH TRADITIONAL PAPER AND PENCIL TESTS, THEY WILL ALSO DEMONSTRATE THEIR LEVEL OF MASTERY THROUGH PERFORMANCE-BASED ASSESSMENT SUCH AS EXHIBITIONS, MULTIPLE VALIDATIONS, PROJECTS AND PORTFOLIOS. THESE DEMONSTRATIONS MIGHT OCCUR IN TRADITIONAL CLASSES, IN EXTRACURRICULAR ACTIVITIES, OR IN THE COMMUNITY. EACH STUDENT'S REPORT CARD WILL DOCUMENT THE STANDARDS THE STUDENT HAS MET INSTEAD OF SIMPLY LISTING THE COURSES TAKEN AND THE GRADE EARNED. THIS TYPE OF ASSESSMENT CREATES AN INTERDEPENDENCE BETWEEN LEARNING THAT IS HANDS-ON AND MINDS-ON. IT HAS IMPRESSIVE POTENTIAL FOR BRINGING INTO CLOSER CORRESPONDENCE THE TASKS AND VALUES OF SCHOOL AND THE WORK PLACE. (ANESSE, DARLING-HAMMOND, 1994)

BALANCING ASSESSMENT

There is no one right way to assess student learning. While performance assessments may tell us how well and deeply student can apply their knowledge, multiple choice tests may be more efficient for determining how well students have knowledge.

Although we present a strong case for performance assessment, all assessments do not need to be this type. Performance assessments offer ways to assess complex thinking and concepts, solving skills and are grounded in realistic problems. A balanced curriculum requires a balanced approached to assessment.

Furthermore, just because an assessment asks students to perform an interesting or complex activity does not make it a good assessment. Assessment must measure something beyond the specific tasks that students are asked to complete. The results of good assessment identify what students can do in a broad knowledge or skill domain. The skills that students exhibit in the assessment situation should transfer to other situations and other problems. (Herman, Aschbacher, Winters)

20

21

DESIGN FIRM | Rapp Collins Communications

ART DIRECTOR/DESIGNER | Amy Usdin

ILLUSTRATOR | Alex Bois

COPYWRITER | Brad Ray

CLIENT | 3M

PAPER/PRINTING | Neenah Environment/Maximum Graphics

The 3M Coping Kit was developed to help employees cope with a difficult corporate restructuring. The kit was distributed by counselors, occupational nurses, and HR managers. In contrast to the somewhat serious subject matter, the graphics and illustrations were bright, playful and inviting, to encourage use of the materials.

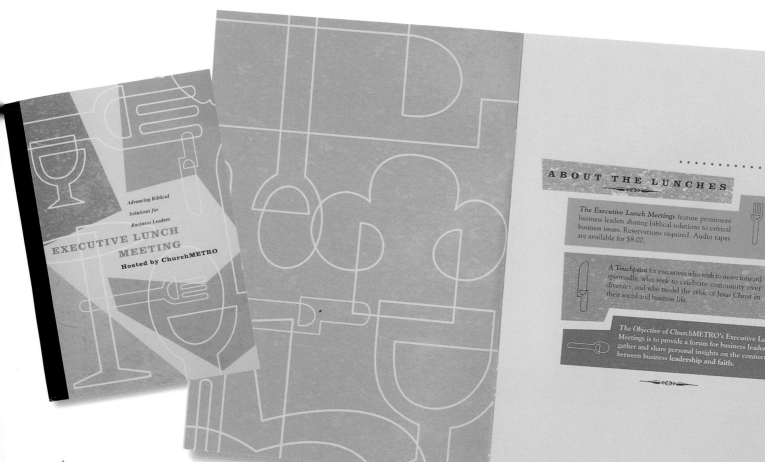

DESIGN FIRM | Design Center

ART DIRECTOR | John Reger

DESIGNER | John Erickson

COPYWRITER | Church Metro

CLIENT | Church Metro

TOOLS | Macintosh, Macromedia FreeHand

PAPER/PRINTING | Warren Lustro/Printcraft

This brochure was mailed to executives and needed to be impressive enough to avoid being categorized as junk mail. It has fun graphics while conveying a serious message.

DESIGN FIRM | University of Iowa
Foundation
ART DIRECTOR/DESIGNER | Dick Blazek
ILLUSTRATOR | Dave Ritter
COPYWRITER | Claudia Reinhardt
CLIENT | Hancher Auditorium—Iowa City
TOOLS | Power Macintosh, Adobe Page-
Maker, Adobe Photoshop
PAPER | Confetti, French Butcher,
Simpson Quest

The client needed an inexpensive
brochure to leave with potential
corporate supporters of the university's
performing-arts auditorium. The
brochure was laser-printed, hand
stamped, and hand assembled in-house
to stay within budgetary limits.

FIRST CLASS

In Direct Mail Promotion

• recognition in special direct mail
campaigns and announcements sent
to subscribers and potential single
ticket purchasers

• supplies of additional performance
literature, when available, for your
organization's own in-house mailings

The White House
1792
1992

USA

DESIGN FIRM | Parham Santana, Inc.

ART DIRECTORS | Millie Hsi, John Parham

DESIGNER | Millie Hsi

COPYWRITER | Diana Amsterdam

CLIENT | VH1

Since the music channel was repositioned as "VH1: Music First," a media and sales kit were developed as "The Source—The Ultimate Guide to VH1 and Music." The source contains programming, demographic information, layers of quotes, inside information, postcards, and a positioning statement to create a rich "everything music" message.

DESIGN FIRM | Teikna

ART DIRECTOR/DESIGNER | Claudia Neri

COPYWRITER | Giovanna Sonnino

CLIENT | Giovanna Sonnino-Planita

TOOLS | QuarkXPress, Adobe Photoshop

PAPER/PRINTING | Fedrigoni/Three-color offset

This brochure is used to promote "Isn't it Romantic?"—an independently made, award-winning Italian film on love and friendship between four characters. The author hands it out at screenings and festivals.

1994 Awards Program

AMERICAN
EXPRESS
QUALITY
PARTNERSHIP
AWARDS

QP 8

American Express Travel Related Services

DESIGN FIRM | J. Graham Hanson Design
DESIGNER | J. Graham Hanson
CLIENT | American Express
TOOLS | QuarkXPress
PAPER/PRINTING | Simpson Starwhite Vicksburg, six PMS colors

An awards booklet designed in 1995 to recognize 1994 winners, each of five winning teams is identified by an individual color designation representing the autonomous and separate nature of each team's accomplishments.

Closing the gap between where we are and where our employees, customers, and shareholders want us to be is a continuous process.

AEQL

American Express Quality Partnerships 8

Unified Customer Service Management System

A powerful combination of world-class service and best-in-class cost efficiency was attained by our Unified Customer Service Management Team (UCSM) when they improved our Risk Management System. The team began by studying the root causes of customer disputes, then designed a program that is better for Cardmembers – and is profit-based.

The new consolidated system resolves more conflicts at the first point of contact, so Cardmembers make fewer calls and receive faster results. This has led to a striking 93% overall satisfaction rating with dispute processing, with 46% of Cardmembers surveyed saying they will use our Card more frequently.

Karen Barlow
Marva Bezabeh
Annette Cardillo
Dan Casper
Shen Yiao Chang
Jean Chong
Damian Davila
Marisa DiLenge
Robin Drews
Ricardo Dumornay
Paula Gosselin
Maria Nastacio
Rick Nowicki
Julieann Pegnataro
Dennis Phelps
Cheryl Potter
John Rathmanner
Arnie Rosentreter
Ray Sharp
Gail Shefield
Dick Spellacy
Michele Stueber
Yang Xu
Pat Yado
Tim Young

American Express Quality Partnerships 8

DESIGN FIRM | Sayles Graphic Design
ART DIRECTOR | John Sayles
DESIGNERS | John Sayles, Jennifer Elliott
ILLUSTRATOR | John Sayles
COPYWRITER | Kristin Lennert
CLIENT | Drake University
PAPER/PRINTING | Curtis Retreeve and chipboard/Offset, screenprinting, and thermography

Using the theme "Be a Part of It," the brochure for Drake University students participating in Greek fraternity and sorority membership uses a double-ply chipboard cover die cut in the shape of a puzzle piece. Inside the piece, a variety of printing and finishing techniques are used for graphics and copy, including thermography, embossing, die cutting, and offset printing. Hand-applied glassine envelopes contain additional information. The brochure is bound with wire-O binding and an aluminum ring.

DESIGN FIRM | Artailor Design House

ART DIRECTOR | Raymond Lam

DESIGNERS | Shirley Wu, Vivian Yao

PHOTOGRAPHER | Dynasty Commercial Photography

CLIENT | Taiwan Securities Co. Ltd.

PRINTER | Zanders

TOOLS | Adobe Illustrator and Adobe Photoshop

The illustration and calligraphy play on both the company's logo and the meaning within Chinese characters. The Chinese character for "money" combines the character for "shell" with the character for "talent." Therefore, this combined graphic of shells (on the left side of the cover) with the Chinese characters for various talents (on the right) presents a subtle but clear visual message to this brochure's predominantly Chinese audience.

DESIGN FIRM | Kan Tai-keung Design & Associates Ltd.

ART DIRECTOR | Kan Tai-keung

DESIGNERS | Kan Tai-keung, Eddy Yu Chi Kong

PHOTOGRAPHER | C.K. Wong

CLIENT | Hong Kong Trade Development Council

PAPER/PRINTER | Coated Art-Paper, Reliance Production

TOOL | Macromedia FreeHand

DESIGN FIRM | Sackett Design Associates

ART DIRECTOR | Mark Sackett

DESIGNERS | Mark Sackett, Wayne Sakamoto

ILLUSTRATOR | Dave Willardson

COPYWRITERS | Brian Belefant, Deborah Benedict, Jim Comparos, Jack Kinney

CLIENT | Lax Magazine

PAPER/PRINTER | Sterling Litho Satin 80 lb., Text Miller Graphics

DESIGN FIRM | Sayles Graphic Design

ART DIRECTOR | John Sayles

DESIGNER | John Sayles

ILLUSTRATOR | John Sayles

COPYWRITER | Wendy Lyons

CLIENT | Cutler Travel Marketing

PAPER/PRINTER | Curtis Paper, Artcraft Printing,
The Printing Station

Printed on text weight paper to save costs, the introductory brochure mails in a glassine envelope. The corporate brochure is a three-dimensional encounter—with foreign coins and stamps, postcards, maps, and travel memorabilia from around the globe, attached by hand to its multi-colored pages.

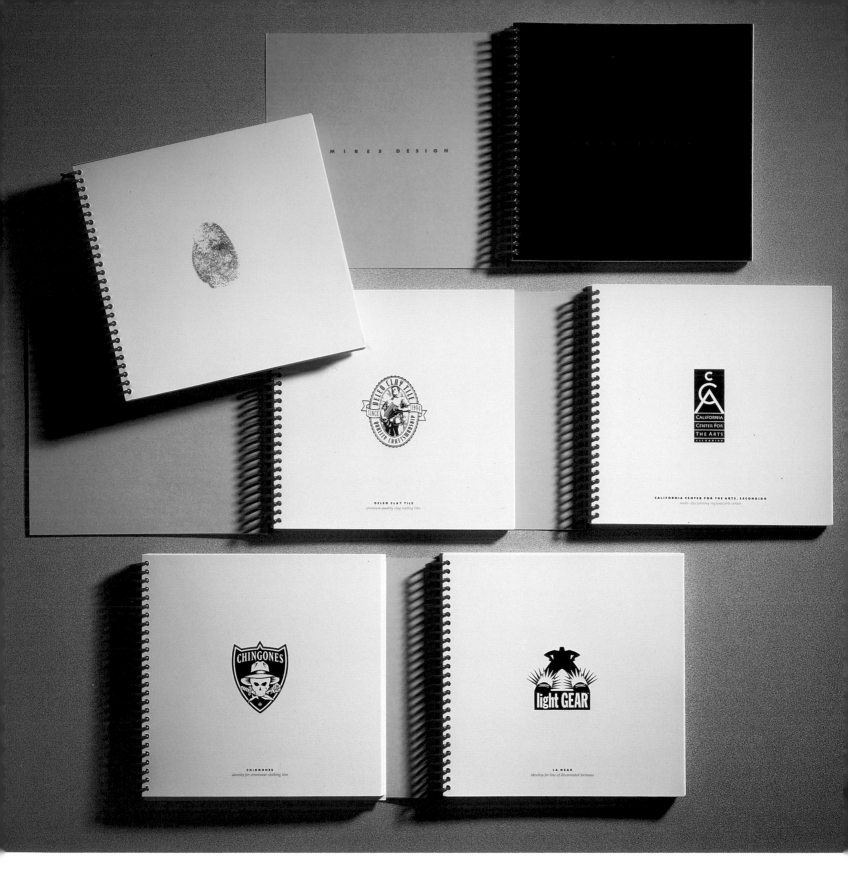

DESIGN FIRM | Mires Design, Inc.
ART DIRECTOR | José Serrano
DESIGNERS | José Serrano, Deborah Fukushima
CLIENT | Mires Design, Inc.

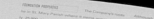

The brochure spread and cover photograph are shown.

DESIGN FIRM | Lee Reedy Design

ART DIRECTOR | Lee Reedy

DESIGNER | Karey Christ-Janer

ILLUSTRATOR | Karey Christ-Janer

PHOTOGRAPHER | Ron Coppock

COPYWRITER | Mark Hellerstein

CLIENT | St. Mary Land & Exploration Co.

PAPER/PRINTER | Centura Dull, L & M Printing

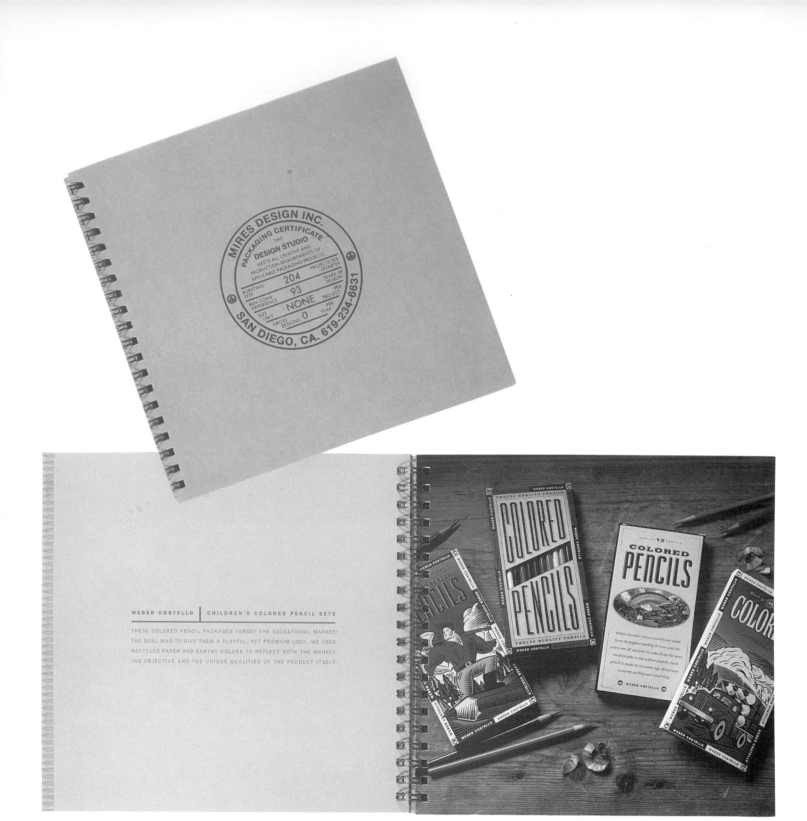

WEBER COSTELLO | CHILDREN'S COLORED PENCIL SETS

THESE COLORED PENCIL PACKAGES TARGET THE EDUCATIONAL MARKET. THE GOAL WAS TO GIVE THEM A PLAYFUL, YET PREMIUM LOOK. WE USED RECYCLED PAPER AND EARTHY COLORS TO REFLECT BOTH THE MARKETING OBJECTIVE AND THE UNIQUE QUALITIES OF THE PRODUCT ITSELF.

DESIGN FIRM | Mires Design
ART DIRECTOR | José Serrano
DESIGNER | José Serrano
CLIENT | Mires Design, Inc.
TOOL | QuarkXPress

This piece uses E Flute cardboard, 4-color offset printing and wire-o binding.

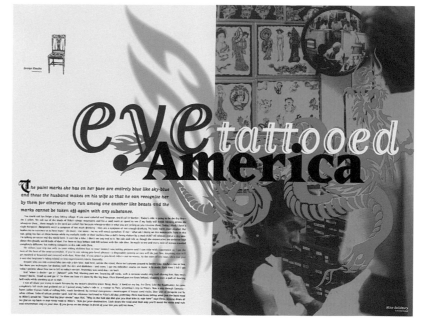

DESIGN FIRM | Mike Salisbury Communications

ART DIRECTOR | Mike Salisbury

DESIGNERS | Mary Evelyn McGough, Sander Van Baalen, Saunder Egging

CLIENT | Stathouse

TOOLS | QuarkXPress, Adobe Photoshop, Adobe Illustrator

1

DESIGN FIRM | Design Ahead

ART DIRECTOR | Ralf Stumpf

DESIGNERS | Stumpf, Decker, Feddeck

ILLUSTRATOR | Ralf Stumpf

CLIENT | Design Ahead

PAPER | Canabis, Ikonofix

TOOLS | Macromedia FreeHand, Adobe Photoshop, and Specular International Infini-D

2

DESIGN FIRM | Held Diedrich

ART DIRECTOR | Dick Held

DESIGNER | Megan Snow

PHOTOGRAPHER | Partners Photography

COPYWRITER | Andie Marshall

CLIENT | Fairbanks Hospital - Annual Report

PAPER/PRINTER | Strathmore Elements

2➤ Fairbanks Hospital is nationally recognized, non-profit, chemical-dependency treatment provider. The theme "Opening Doors to Recovery" is visually carried through this brochure with photographs of actual doors. Since the clients are a not-for-profit entity, wise budget management dictated the use of three spot colors throughout the piece.

1

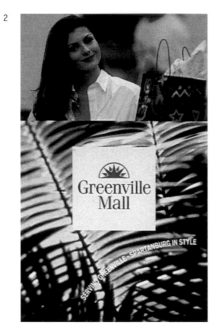

Greenville Mall

SERVING GREENVILLE-SPARTANBURG IN STYLE

2

THE BEAUTY OF SOUTHERN GARDENS

Located in the heart of the Greenville-Spartanburg-Anderson Metropolitan Area, Greenville Mall is setting a new standard in style for South Carolina. The expanded and renovated 700,000 square-foot mall will open in the summer of 1995 as the most dynamic shopping center in the state's fastest growing market.

Three anchor department stores: Parisian, J.B. White, Montgomery Ward (and a planned fourth department store), an exciting collection of upscale fashion and specialty shops, a new food court and a number of full-service restaurants will attract fashion-conscious shoppers from throughout this growing region.

1

DESIGN FIRM | Segura Inc.

ART DIRECTOR | Carlos Segura

DESIGNER | Carlos Segura

PHOTOGRAPHER | Geof Kern

COPYWRITER | John Cleland

CLIENT | John Cleland

PRINTER | Argus Press

TOOLS | Adobe Illustrator, QuarkXPress, and Adobe Photoshop

2

DESIGN FIRM | Gregory Group

ART DIRECTOR | Jon Gregory

CLIENT | Intershop Real Estate

PAPER/PRINTER | Loe 100 lb. Cover Gloss, Colormark

TOOLS | QuarkXPress

2► Created for a large regional mall undergoing a major renovation, this leasing brochure had to be upscale and vibrant, to motivate tenant interest. A blend of fashion-forward photos and detail photos of gifts and food sets the tone for the mall's new direction.

DESIGN FIRM | Grand Design Co.

ART DIRECTORS | Grand So, Kwong Chi Man

DESIGNERS | Kwong Chi Man, Grand So

ILLUSTRATOR | Martin Ng

PHOTOGRAPHER | Almond Chu

COPYWRITER | Finny Maddess Consultants Ltd.

CLIENT | Sureap Ltd.

PRINTER | Reliance Production

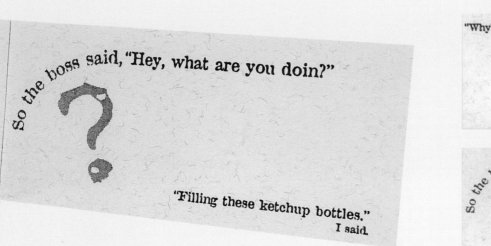

"Really?" she said.

"Yeah, kinda slow. No customers." I said.

Shari Flack
Waitress
Age 17

So the boss said, "Hey, what are you doin?"

"Sweeping the floor."
I said.

"Why?" he asked.

"Phone's not ringing." I said.

Shari Flack
Receptionist
Age 19

So the boss said, "Hey, what are you doin?"

"Couple of house ads."
I said.

"Why?" he asked.

"Finished those other jobs." I said.

Shari Flack
Graphic Designer
Age 25

No slouch. Mover. Achiever. Put me on the payroll.
Shari Flack · P.O. Box 1354 · Pacifica, CA 94044 · (415) 355-2067

So the boss said, "Hey, what are you doin?"

"Filling these ketchup bottles."
I said.

DESIGN FIRM | Shari Flack

ART DIRECTOR | Shari Flack

DESIGNER | Shari Flack

COPYWRITER | Shari Flack

CLIENT | Shari Flack

PAPER | Arvey

TOOL | QuarkXPress

Used as a follow-up piece for résumés, this brochure was photocopied in-house to save costs, then assembled by hand.

DESIGN FIRM | Eskind Waddell
ART DIRECTOR | Roslyn Eskind
DESIGNERS | Roslyn Eskind and Nicola Lyon
ILLUSTRATOR | Franklin Hammond
COPYWRITER | Toronto Dominion Bank
CLIENT | Toronto Dominion Bank
PRINTER | Arthurs - Jones Lithographing Ltd.
TOOLS | Adobe Illustrator, QuarkXPress, and Adobe Photoshop

The report is organized in tiered, manageable sections, with varying amounts of detail and complexity—so it appeals to a variety of audiences.

DESIGN FIRM | 246 Fifth Design

ART DIRECTOR | Terry Laurenzio

DESIGNER | Sid Lee

COPYWRITER | Joy Parks

CLIENT | 246 Fifth Design

PAPER/PRINTER | Neenah, Custom Printers of Renfrew

TOOL | Adobe Illustrator

This piece features 5-color metallic ink on black linen paper, with a 2-color interior. Some of the type is hand drawn.

1

DESIGN FIRM | Masterline Communications Ltd.
ART DIRECTORS | Grand So, Raymond Au,
   Kwong Chi Man, Candy Chan
DESIGNERS | Grand So, Raymond Au,
   Kwong Chi Man
ILLUSTRATORS | Grand So, Kwong Chi Man
PHOTOGRAPHER | David Lo
COPYWRITERS | Grand So, Johnson Cheng
CLIENT | Masterline Communications Ltd.

2

DESIGN FIRM | Grand Design Co.
ART DIRECTORS | Grand So, C.M. Kwong,
   Raymond Au, Candy Chan
DESIGNERS | Grand So, C.M. Kwong,
   Raymond Au
ILLUSTRATORS | Grand So, C.M. Kwong
PHOTOGRAPHER | David Lo
COPYWRITERS | Grand So, Mimi Lee
CLIENT | Grand Design Co.

2► The portraits on the front and inside
   covers are designed to reflect the
   intelligence and energy
   of the client.

2

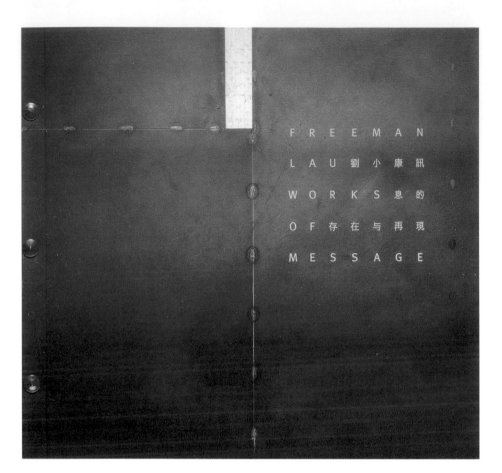

FREEMAN
LAU 劉 小 康 訊
WORKS 息 的
OF 存 在 与 再 現
MESSAGE

DESIGN FIRM | Kan & Lau Design Consultants
ART DIRECTOR/DESIGNER | Lau Siu Hong
TOOLS | Adobe PageMaker, Macromedia FreeHand,
Adobe Photoshop

The artwork in the Works of Message were inspired by
books but without words.

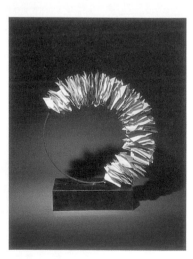

inscrutable.
As a professional designer and
amateur artist, Lau's "amateur
work" in recent years might be
comparable to the work of many
"professional" artists. The
concepts and the details of his
design works, which I have seen,
testify to his mastery of design
vocabulary as well as the clarity
and variety of his ideas. It is
therefore all the more striking that
he should be so single-minded in
the choice of content and form of

DESIGN FIRM | KMPH Fox 26

DESIGN DIRECTOR | Rebecca M. Barnes

COMPUTER PRODUCTION | Mullins and Son

PRINTING PROCESS | Four-color process

The designers began with the traditional folder to present
an annual sports package designed to help their Marketing
Department with client presentations. A separate one-sheet
insert is held inside the folder, so the folder can be used
throughout the year.

DESIGN FIRM | Roslyn Eskind Associates Limited
ART DIRECTOR | Roslyn Eskind
DESIGNERS | Roslyn Eskind, Heike Sillaste, Gary Mansbridge
COPYWRITER | Roslyn Eskind
CLIENT | Services Group of America
TOOLS | QuarkXPress, Adobe Illustrator and Photoshop
PAPER | Horizon 8pt. cover dull
PRINTING PROCESS | Heidelberg (direct to plate)

Contact

Roslyn Eskind Associates Limited

Eskind

Associates

@

471 Richmond Street West   Suite 200
Toronto, Ontario   M5V 1X9

Graphic Design
Consultants

For..

tel   416 504 6075
fax   416 504 6085
email   @roslyneskind.com

João Machado

Cartazes

DESIGN FIRM | João Machado, Design Lda.
ALL DESIGN | João Machado
TOOLS | Macromedia FreeHand, QuarkXPress

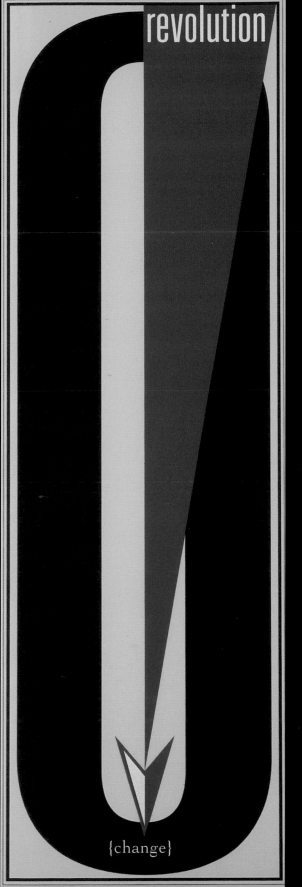

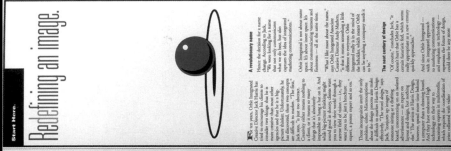

DESIGN FIRM | Orbit Integrated

ART DIRECTOR/DESIGNER | Jack Harris

ILLUSTRATORS | Jack Harris, Emory Au

COPYWRITER | William Harris

CLIENT | Orbit Integrated

TOOLS | QuarkXPress, Adobe Illustrator and Photoshop

PAPER | 80 lb. Mohawk Poseidon Cover

PRINTING PROCESS | Four-color offset

This is a vehicle for the marketing communications firm
to announce its name change, and to provide its clients
with a taste of its marketing and branding philosophies,
in a format that commands attention.

DESIGN FIRM | Mires Design
ART DIRECTOR | John Ball
DESIGNER | Gale Spitzley
ILLUSTRATORS | Miquel Perez, Jeff Samaripa
COPYWRITER | Brian Woosley
TOOLS | QuarkXPress, Adobe Illustrator
PAPER | Zanders Mirricard silver, cover; 12 pt. Zanders
         Chromolux Vario Cover, red, interior
PRINTING PROCESS | Four-color offset

The Mires Design identity book is used to present their
work to potential clients, both in person and via direct
mail. The designer used a mirror-like cover stock to reflect
the firm's philosophy on corporate and brand identity.

DESIGN FIRM | ZGraphics, Ltd.
ART DIRECTOR | Joe Zeller
DESIGNER | Gregg Rojewski
ILLUSTRATOR | Paul Turnbaugh

Jelly beans for the holiday season! What could be more yummy? ZGraphics' greeting card emphasizes the jelly bean theme by using photos of actual jelly beans in conjunction with illustrations of the holiday season.

VOIT SPORTS | **THE ORB BASKETBALL**

IT'S A WHOLE NEW KIND OF BASKETBALL. A DIMPLED PRACTICE
BALL DESIGNED TO HELP AVERAGE-SIZED HANDS PLAY MORE
LIKE NBA-SIZED HANDS. IN ADDITION TO NAMING THE PRODUCT,
WE CREATED A UNIQUE IDENTITY AND PACKAGING THAT GIVES
CONSUMERS AN INSTANT GRIP ON WHAT THIS BALL'S ALL ABOUT.

DESIGN FIRM | Mires Design

ART DIRECTOR | Jose A. Serrano

DESIGNERS | Deborah Hom, Gale Spitzley

COPYWRITER | John Kuraoka, Brian Woosley

TOOLS | QuarkXPress

PRINTING PROCESS | Four-color offset

This promotion was created to showcase Mires Design's
latest packaging projects. Their strategy was to present
the work in a format that made use of corrugated board
to give a tactile feel and make the book memorable.

DESIGN FIRM | Architectural Brochures
ART DIRECTOR | Liza Bachrach
ALL DESIGN | Liza Bachrach
TOOLS | QuarkXPress, Adobe Illustrator
PAPER | Gilclear, oxford, white 28 lb.
PRINTING PROCESS | Four PMS colors

The firm wanted a brochure that would demonstrate to the public all the wonderful design options there are for brochures: color, unique paper, emboss, dye cut, score, fold, and bleed. They created a design that coordinates well with their letterhead, and is simple, yet elegant.

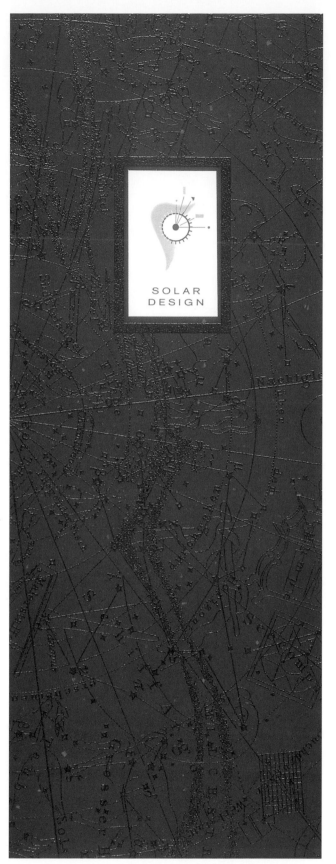

DESIGN FIRM | Solar Design

ART DIRECTOR | Jennifer Schmidt

DESIGNERS | Jennifer Schmidt, Susan Russell

TOOLS | QuarkXPress, Adobe Illustrator and Photoshop

PAPER | Cover: Fox River Confetti;
interior: Neenah Classic Crest

PRINTING PROCESS | Black thermography, cover;
two-color PMS, interior

This brochure educates the reader on the process of design and is one component of the firm's presentation folder. Sun facts are included to reinforce the firm's goal; to give each client Solar's energy!

DESIGN FIRM | Sayles Graphic Design

ART DIRECTOR/DESIGNER | John Sayles

PHOTOGRAPHER | Bill Nellans

COPYWRITER | Wendy Lyons

PAPER | Crown Vantage Terracoat Gray

PRINTING PROCESS | Offset

Sayles and Clark commemorated the airing of a promotional TV show with a special announcement. The accordion-fold mailer, appropriately titled Our Next Project Is on the House, is reminiscent of a wallet full of photos. A dozen detailed shots display their eye-catching collections, showcasing their appreciation for the elegance and style of the Art Deco era.

DESIGN FIRM | Marketing and Communication Strategies, Inc.

ART DIRECTOR | Eric Dean Freese

DESIGNERS | Chris Weaver, Eric Dean Freese, Marc Valenta

PHOTOGRAPHERS | MCS Staff

COPYWRITERS | MCS Staff

TOOLS | Adobe Photoshop and Illustrator, QuarkXPress

PAPER | Evergreen 100 lb. cover, Utopia 2 Dull, Glama

PRINTING PROCESS | Two-color plus spot varnish on cover

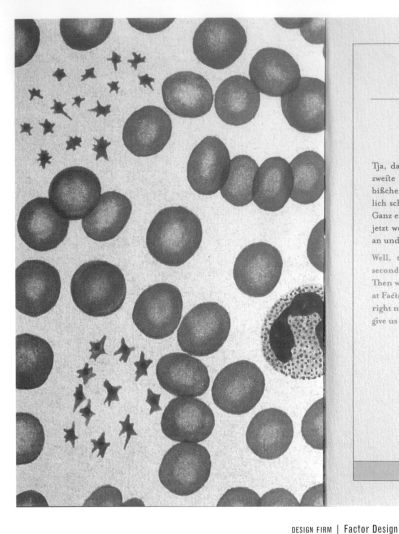

FACTOR DESIGN   FACTOR DESIGN

über neugierde on curiosity

Tja, das war er, der erste Eindruck, für den es keine zweite Chance gibt. Wir hoffen, wir konnten Sie ein bißchen neugierig machen. Da hätten wir dann nämlich schon eine gemeinsame Basis. Wir sind neugierig. Ganz enorm sogar. Und ganz besonders darauf, was Sie jetzt wohl über uns denken. Rufen Sie uns doch mal an und erzählen Sie es uns. Sprechen wir über Details.

Well, that was it—the first impression. There's no second chance. We hope we've made you a bit curious. Then we already have something in common. Because at Factor Design, we're extremely curious. For example, right now we're wondering what you think of us. Why not give us a call and let us know?

BILDTAFEL/PLATE 07 LEUKOZYTEN   **13**

DESIGN FIRM | Factor Design

ART DIRECTOR | Olaf Stein

DESIGNER | Eva Ralle

ILLUSTRATOR | Stock

PHOTOGRAPHER | Frank Stöckel

COPYWRITER | Hannah S. Fricke

TOOLS | Macromedia FreeHand, QuarkXPress

PAPER | Romerturn Esparto

PRINTING PROCESS | Four-color offset

This brochure is part of Factor's self promotional piece that tells clients about the firm's general philosophy on graphic design.

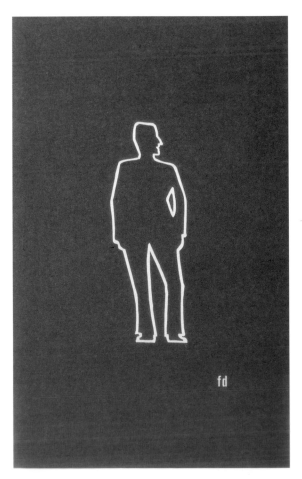

I D E A   B O O K   4 . 0

DESIGN FIRM | Caesar Photo Design, Inc.
ART DIRECTOR | Caesar Lima
DESIGNERS | Caesar Lima, Pouane Dinso
PHOTOGRAPHER | Caesar Lima
COPYWRITER | Jennifer Castle
PRINTING PROCESS | 5/5 colors

Since Caesar Photo Design is a 100% digital photo studio, they wanted to display a futuristic image to potential clients. This brochure eliminated the need to send portfolios of their photographic work, because it speaks for itself: big images and few words are key elements of its success.

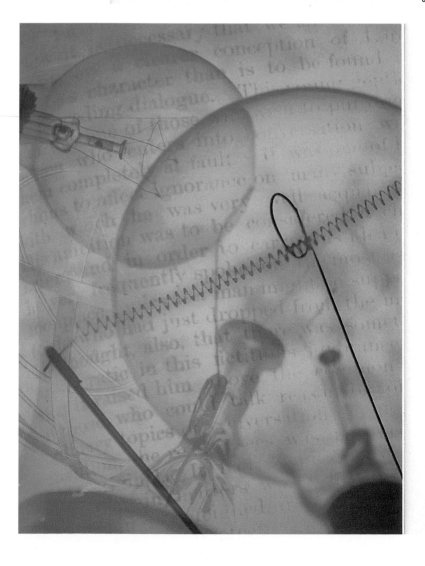

Beyond the hum of the computer,

beyond the glare of the screen...

There is always the art.

Software can not generate creativity.

Without the idea, there is no image

Without the idea, there is nothing...

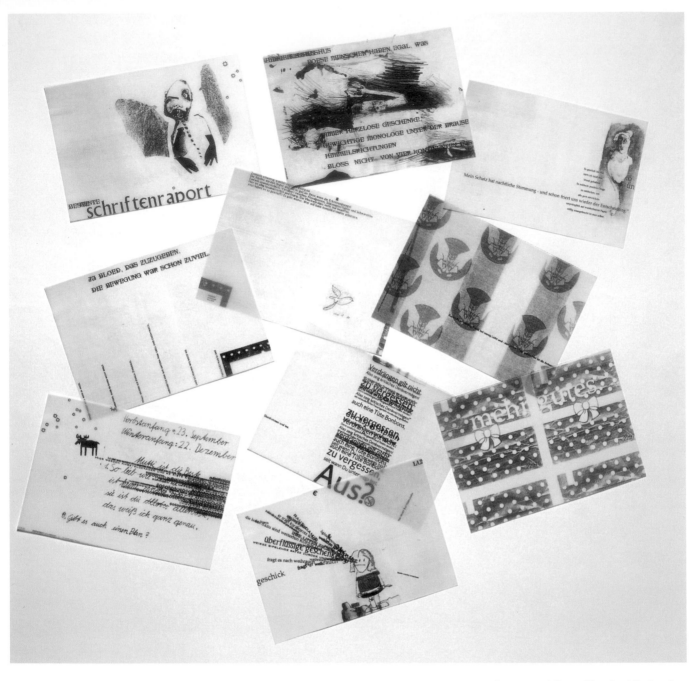

DESIGNERS/ILLUSTRATORS | Doreen Kiepsel and Marlena Sang
COPYWRITERS | Doreen Kiepsel and Marlena Sang
PRINTING PROCESS | Inkjet and photocopier

Ten sheets were put together in one piece to create Christmas greetings that use the designers' own illustrations, texts, forms, and fonts. The recipient can pick the one he or she likes best and just enjoy it.

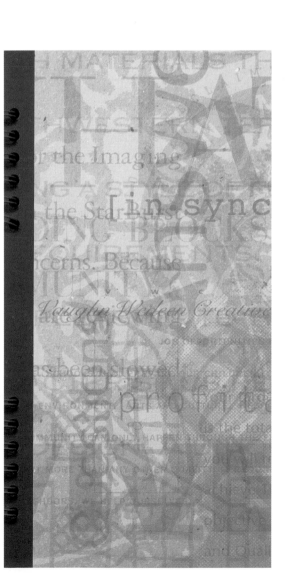

■ NATIONAL INSTITUTIONAL PHARMACY SERVICES INC. These sales materials were part of a corporate identity program for a provider of pharmaceutical products and services for nursing care facilities.

■ DANCING DESERT PRESS This logo was designed to capture the whim and whimsy of this small Southwest publishing company which specialized in consumer-friendly alternative shopping guides.

■ U S WEST COMMUNICATIONS "Ain't It Grand" was one of a series of internal sales promotions that operated under an overall communications strategy of "Making Music Together". This campaign included sales kits, posters, campaign collateral and silkscreened apparel.

DESIGN FIRM | Vaughn Wedeen Creative
ART DIRECTORS/DESIGNERS | Rick Vaughn, Steve Wedeen
ILLUSTRATOR | Kristi Carter
PHOTOGRAPHERS | Dave Nufer, Michael Barley
COPYWRITER | Steve Wedeen
TOOLS | QuarkXPress, Adobe Photoshop,
        Macromedia FreeHand

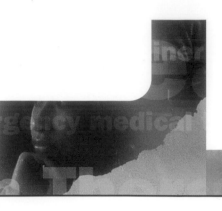

DIRECTORY

246 FIFTH DESIGN
1379 Bank
Ottawa, Ontario K1H 8N3
CANADA

ADELE BASS & CO. DESIGN
758 E. Colorado Boulevard
Suite 209
Pasadena, CA 91101

AERIAL
58 Federal Street
San Francisco, CA 94107

ALAN CHAN DESIGN COMPANY
2/F Shiu Lam Building
23 Laurd Road
Wanchai, HONG KONG

ANDERSON THOMAS DESIGN INC.
110 29th Avenue North
Suite 301
Nashville, TN 37203

ANDREAS WEISS
Moltkestrasse 7
28203 Bremen, Graf
GERMANY

ARCHITECTURAL BROCHURES
7 Clove Court
South Elgin, IL 60177

ARTAILOR DESIGN HOUSE
4th Floor, 414
Section 4
Shin Yi Road
Taipei, TAIWAN R.O.C.

ATELIER GRAPHIQUE BIZART
20 Rue J. P. Beicht
L-1226 LUXEMBOURG

AWG GRAPHICS COMUNICAÇÃO LTDA
R. Maestro Cardim, 377
8 and Saspulao
Sao Paulo, BRAZIL

B2 DESIGN
220 South 5th Street
Dekalb, IL 60115

BARBARA BROWN MARKETING AND DESIGN
792 Colina Vista
Ventura, CA 93003

BARRY HUTZEL
2058 Breeze Drive
Holland, MI 49424

BELYEA DESIGN ALLIANCE
1809 7th Avenue
Suite 1007
Seattle, WA 98101

BIG EYE CREATIVE, INC.
1300 Richards Street
Suite 101
Vancouver, BC V6B 3G6
CANADA

BLACK CAT DESIGN
637 3rd Avenue
Seattle, WA 98119

BLUESTONE DESIGN
87 Mannamead Road
Plymouth, Devon
ENGLAND

BRABENDERCOX
2100 Wharton Street
Pittsburgh, PA 15203

BREVIS/KD COMPUTER GRAPHICS
Otto-Sadlerstrasse 4
33100 Padrborn
GERMANY

BULLET COMMUNICATIONS, INC.
200 South Midland Avenue
Joliet, IL 60426

CAESAR PHOTO DESIGN, INC.
21358 Nordhoff Street
#107
Chatsworth, CA 91311

CALDERA DESIGN
1201 East Jefferson, #A25
Phoenix, AZ 85034

CATO DERRO DISENO
Estanislao Diaz 102 (1642)
San Isidro, Buenos Aires
ARGENTENIA

CATO DESIGN INC.
254 Swan Street
Richmond
3121 AUSTRALIA

CARMICHAEL LYNCH
800 Hennepin Avenue
Minneapolis, MN 55403

CLARK DESIGN
444 Spear Street
Suite 210
San Francisco, CA 94105

COMMUNICATION ARTS COMPANY
129 East Pascaquola Street
Jackson, MS 39201

CORNOYER-HEDRICK, INC.
2425 East Camelback Road
Suite 400
Phoenix, AZ 85016

CREATIVE CONSPIRACY, INC.
110 East 9th Street
Durango, CO 81301

THE CREATIVE RESPONSE CO., INC.
217 Nicanor Garcia Street
Bel-Air II, Makati City
PHILIPPINES

THE CRITERION GROUP
12 Piedmont Center
Suite 100
Atlanta, GA 30308

DAMEON HICKMAN DESIGN
1801 Dove
#104
Newport Beach, CA 92660

DANIEL BASTIAN
Moltkestrasse 7
28203 Bremen, Graf
GERMANY

DAVID CARTER DESIGN
4112 Swiss Avenue
Dallas, TX 75204

DENISE KEMPER DESIGN
505 Wintergreen Drive
Wadsworth, OH 44281

DEPARTMENT 058
Leo Pharmaceuticals
Industri Parken 55
DK-2750
DENMARK

DESIGN AHEAD
Kirchfeldstrasse 16
45219 Essen-Kettwig
GERMANY

DESIGN CENTER
15119 Minnetonka Boulevard
Minnetonka, MN 55345

THE DESIGN GROUP
Sagmeister, Inc.
222 West 14th Street
New York, NY 10011

DESIGN GUYS
119 North Fourth Street
#400
Minneapolis, MN 55401

DIA
Central House, Alwyne Road
London JW19 7AB
UNITED KINGDOM

DOREEN KIEPSEL AND MARLENA SANG
Lornsenstr. 36
22767 Hamburg
GERMANY

ELTON WARD DESIGN
P.O. Box 802
Parramatta
NSW 2124, AUSTRALIA

EMERSON, WAJDOWICZ STUDIOS
1123 Broadway
Suite 1106
New York, NY 10010

ESKIND WADDELL
471 Richmond Street West
Toronto, Ontario M5V 1X9
CANADA

FACTOR DESIGN
Schulterblatt 58
20357 Hamburg
GERMANY

FERNÀNDEZ DESIGN
920 North Franklin Street
Suite 303
Chicago, IL 60610

GEORGE TSCHERNY
238 East 72nd Street
New York, NY 10021

GIORGIO ROCCO COMMUNICATIONS
Design Consultants
Via Domenichino 27
20149 Milano
ITALY

GOODHUE & ASSOCIATES DESIGN
COMMUNICATION
465 McGill Street
8th Floor
Montreal, QB H2
CANADA

GRAFIK COMMUNICATIONS, LTD.
1199 North Fairfax Street
#700
Alexandria, VA 22314

GRAND DESIGN COMPANY
Rm 1901, Valley Centre
80-82 Morrison Hill Road
Wanchai, HONG KONG

GREGORY GROUP
2811 McKinney
Suite 216
Dallas, TX 75204

GRETEMAN GROUP
142 North Mosley
Wichita, KS 67202

GRIFFIN DESIGN
RR 22 Box 6
Bloomington, IL 61701

HELD DIEDRICH, INC.
703 East 30th
Suite 16
Indianapolis, IN 46205

HORNALL ANDERSON DESIGN WORKS,
INC.
1008 Western Avenue
Suite 600
Seattle, WA 98104

IMPRESS SAS
Via Galimberti 18
13051 Biella
ITALY

INLAND GROUP, INC.
22a north Main
Edwardsville, IL 62025

INSIGHT DESIGN COMMUNICATIONS
322 South Mosley
Wichita, KS 67202

INTEGRATED MARKETING SERVICES
279 Wall Street
Princeton, NJ 08540

J. GRAHAM HANSON DESIGN
307 E. 89th Street
#6G
New York, NY 10128

JD THOMAS COMPANY
820 Monroe
#333
Grand Rapids, MI 49503

JEFF FISHER LOGO MOTIVES
P.O. Box 6631
Portland, OR 97228-6631

JOÃO MACHADO DESIGN LDA
Ria Padre Xavier Coltinho
#125
4150 Porto
PORTUGAL

JOHNSON GRAPHICS
2 Riverfront
Newbury, MA 01951

JOSEPH RATTAN DESIGN
5924 Pebblestone Lane
Plano, TX 75093

JUICE DESIGN
1572 Howard Street
San Francisco, CA 94103

KAISERDICKEN
149 Cherry Street
Burlington, VT 05401

KAN & LAU DESIGN CONSULTANTS
28/F Great Smart Tower
230 Wanchai Road
HONG KONG

KAN TAI-KEUNG DESIGN & ASSOCIATES
LTD.
28/F Great Smart Tower
230 Wanchai Road
HONG KONG

KBB COMMUNICATIONS DESIGN
49 River Street
Suite 2
Waltham, MA 02154

KEN WEIGHTMAN DESIGN
7036 Park Drive
New Port Richey, FL 34652

KIMBERLY COOKE AND ANN FREERKS
631 East Jefferson Street
Iowa City, IA 52245

KMPH FOX
5111 East McKinley Avenue
Fresno, CA 93727

LABBÉ DESIGN CO.
20 Executive Park
Suite 200
Irvine, CA 92614

LEE REEDY CREATIVE, INC.
1542 Williams Street
Denver, CO 80218

THE KUESTER GROUP
81 South 9th Street
Suite 300
Minneapolis, MN 55402

THE LEONHARDT GROUP
1218 Third Avenue
#620
Seattle, WA 98101

LIGATURE, INC.
165 North Canal
Chicago, IL 60606

LOUISA SUGAR DESIGN
1650 Jackson Street
Suite 307
San Francisco, CA 94109

M & COMPANY
Sagmeister, Inc.
222 West 19th Street
New York, NY 10011

MAMMOLITI CHAN DESIGN
P.O. Box 6097
Melbourne, 8008
AUSTRALIA

MARC MARAHRENS
Flotowstrasse 14
22083 Hamburg
GERMANY

MARKETING AND COMMUNICATIONS
STRATEGIES, INC.
2218 1ST Avenue NE
Cedar Rapids, IA 52402

MARLENA SANG
Lornsenstr. 36
22767 Hamburg
GERMANY

MARTINROSS DESIGN
1125 Xerxes Avenue South
Minneapolis, MN 55405

MASON CHARLES DESIGN
147 West 38th Street
New York, NY 10018

MASTERLINE COMMUNICATIONS LTD.
Rm 1902, Valley Centre
80-82 Morrison Hill Road
Wanchai, HONG KONG

MCCULLOUGH CREATIVE GROUP, INC.
890 Iowa Street
Dubuque, IA 52001

MELISSA PASSEHL DESIGN
1275 Lincoln Avenue #7
San Jose, CA 95125

MENDIOLA DESIGN STUDIO
Calle 37 #523 Mercedes
Buenos Aires, ARGENTINA

MERVIL PAYLOR DESIGN
1917 Lennox Avenue
Charlotte, NC 28203

METALLI LINDBERG ADVERTISING
Via Garibaldi 5/D
31015 Conegliano (Treviso)
ITALY

METROPOLIS CORPORATION
56 Broad Street
Milford, CT 06460

MICHAEL COURTNEY DESIGN
121 East Boston
Seattle, WA 98102

MIKE SALISBURY COMMUNICATIONS,
INC.
2200 Amapola Court
Suite 202
Torrance, CA 90501

MIRES DESIGN, INC.
2345 Kettner Boulevard
San Diego, CA 92101

MORGAN DESIGN STUDIO, INC.
345 Whitehall Street Southwest
Suite 106
Atlanta, GA 30303

MULLER AND COMPANY
4739 Belleview
Kansas City, MO 64112

NESNADNY AND SWARTZ
10803 Magnolia Drive
Cleveland, OH 44106

OAKLEY DESIGN STUDIOS
519 SW Park Avenue
Suite 521
Portland, OR 97205

ORBIT INTEGRATED
722 Yorklyn Road
Hockessin, DE 19707

PALMQUIST AND PALMQUIST
P.O. Box 325
Bozeman, MT 59771

PARHAM SANTANA, INC. 233
7 West 18th Street
New York, NY 10011

PENSARE DESIGN GROUP LTD.
729 15th Street, N.W.
1st Floor
Washington, D.C. 20005

PEPE GIMENO, SL
C/Cadirers, SN
46110 Godella
Valencia, SPAIN

PINKHAUS DESIGN
2424 South Dixie Highway
Suite 201
Miami, FL 33133

PLAYBOY ENTERPRISES
Marise Mizrahi GWTS
565 5TH Avenue
New York, NY 10017

POLIVKA LOGAN DESIGN (PLD)
411 North Washington
Minneapolis, MN 55402

PRICE LEARMAN ASSOCIATES
737 Market Street
Kirkland, WA 98033

PROSPERA
8400 Normandale Lake Boulevard
Minneapolis, MN 55437

Q DESIGN NEUBERG 14
65193 Wiesbaden
GERMANY

RAMONA HUTKO DESIGN
4712 South Chelsea Lane
Bethesda, MD 20814

RAPP COLLINS COMMUNICATIONS
901 Marquette Avenue
17th Floor
Minneapolis, MN 55402

RAVEN MADD DESIGN
P.O. Box 11-331
Wellington
NEW ZEALAND

RENATE GOKL
803 South Coler Avenue
#5
Urbana, IL 61801

REVOLUZION
Uhlandstrasse 4
78579 Neuhausen ob Eck
GERMANY

RICHARD ENDLY DESIGN, INC.
510 First Avenue
Suite 206
Minneapolis, MN 55403

THE RIORDAN DESIGN GROUP, INC.
131 George Street
Oakville, Ontario L68 3B9
CANADA

ROSE SREBRO DESIGN
140 Carlton Road
Newton, MA 02168

ROSLYN ESKIND ASSOCIATES LIMITED
471 Richmond Street
Toronto, Ontario MSV 1X9
CANADA

SACKETT DESIGN ASSOCIATES
2103 Scott Street
San Francisco, CA 94115-2120

SAGMEISTER, INC.
222 West 14th Street
New York, NY 10011

SAYLES GRAPHIC DESIGN
308 Eighth Street
Des Moines, IA 50309

SEGURA INC.
361 West Chestnut Street
1st Floor
Chicago, IL 60610

SHARI FLACK
P.O. Box 1354
Pacifica, CA 94044

SHIELDS DESIGN
415 East Olive Avenue
Fresno, CA 93728

SIBLEY/PETEET DESIGN
3232 McKinney
#1200
Dallas, TX 75204

SILICON GRAPHICS CREATIVE
601 Minnesota
#120
San Francisco, CA 94107

SJI ASSOCIATES
1133 Broadway
Suite 635
New York, NY 10010

SOLAR DESIGN
1225 West Oakton Street
Arlington Heights, IL 60004

SOMMESE DESIGN
481 Glenn Road
State College, PA 16803

SOUND TRANSIT
1100 2nd Avenue
#500
Seattle, WA 98101-3423

SOVEREIGN CREATIVE GROUP, INC.
P.O. Box 194543
Hatoreysta, S. J. 00919-4543
PUERTO RICO

STOLTZE DESIGN
49 Melcher Street
Boston, MA 02210

STUDIO MD
1512 Alaskan Way
Seattle, WA 98101

STUDIO W, INC.
17 Vestry Street
Ground Floor
New York, NY 10013

SULLIVAN PERKINS
2811 McKinney
Suite 201
Dallas, TX 75204

SWIETER DESIGN U.S.
3227 McKinney Avenue
Suite 201
Dallas, TX 75204

TANAGRAM
855 W. Blackhawk Street
Chicago, IL 60622

TEIKNA
366 Adelaide Street East
541 Toronto, Ontario M5A 3X9
CANADA

TELEVISION BROADCASTS LIMITED
TV City
Clear Water Bay Road
Kowloon, HONG KONG

TGD COMMUNICATIONS
1420 Print Street
#210
Alexandria, VA 22314

TOM FOWLER, INC.
9 Webbs Hill Road
Stamford, CT 06903

TONI SCHOWALTER DESIGN
1133 Broadway
Suite 1610
New York, NY 10010

UNIVERSITY OF IOWA FOUNDATION
P.O. Box 4550
Iowa City, IA 552244-4550

VARDIMON DESIGN
87 Shlomo Hamelech Street
Tel Aviv 64512
ISRAEL

VAUGHN WEDEEN CREATIVE
407 Rio Grande NM
Albuquerque, NM 87104

VISUAL MARKETING ASSOCIATES
322 South Patterson Boulevard
Dayton, OH 45402

W DESIGN, INC.
411 Washington Avenue North
Suite 104
Minneapolis, MN 55401

WEHRMAN & COMPANY, INC.
8175 Big Bend Boulevard
Suite 250
St. Louis, MO 63119

WERK-HAUS
22-2 Plaza Damansara
Medan Setia 2, Bukit Damansara
Kuala Lumpur
MALAYSIA

WIDMEYER DESIGN
911 Western Avenue
#305
Seattle, WA 98104

WITHERSPOON ADVERTISING
1000 W. Weatherford
Fort Worth, TX 76102

WOLFRAM RESEARCH, INC.
100 Trade Center Drive
Champaign, IL 61820

WOOD DESIGN
1775 York Avenue 326
New York, NY 10128

WOOD DESIGN AND ART STUDIO
15371 Locust Street
Omaha, NE 68116

WORDS OF ART
2346 Echo Hills Circle
Atlanta, GA 30345

X DESIGN COMPANY
2525 West Main Street
#201
Littleton, CO 44126

Z GRAPHICS LTD.
322 North River Street
East Dundee, IL 60118

ZYLSTRA DESIGN
50575 W 220th Street
Fairview Park, OH 44126

INDEX